1943

THE NEWS
THE EVENTS
AND
THE LIVES
OF 1943

Elizabeth Absalom & Malcolm Watson

D'Azur Publishing

Published by D'Azur Publishing 2023
D'Azur Publishing is a Division of D'Azur Limited

First published in Great Britain in 2023 by D'Azur Limited
Contact: info@d-azur.com Visit www.d-azur.com
ISBN 9798367076653

ACKNOWLEDGEMENTS
The publisher wishes to acknowledge the following people and sources:

British Newspaper Archive; The Times Archive; Cover Malcolm Watson; p4 United States Library of Congress's Prints and Photographs division; p4 Derby Telegraph Bygones; p4 Forces War Records; p8 Malcolm Watson; p9 Chemical Engineer; p12 GaryReggae; p25 girlsatwar.com; http://www.bushywood.com; p27 sallyantiques.co.uk; p27 Wartime Information Board, CC0, via Wikimedia Commons; p29 Imperial War Museum; p29 qmsmilitaria.com; p31 National Army Museum; p31 M Arnol; p33 epicmilitaria.com; p33 Imperial War Museum; p35 foodandcity: p39 fet.uwe.ac.uk; p41 rarenewspapers.com' p51 Crown Content, Royal Armouries; p53 National Maritime Museum; p55 London Coins; p57 Tagishsimon; p59 Historic Royal Palaces; p59 Constable50806; p61 warhistoryonline.com; p67 Detmar Owen; p69 Wisdom learning; p73 Mick R; p75 thepilgrimtrust.org.uk; p77 a-e-g.org.uk; p79 portsmouth.co.uk; p81 vintagenewsdaily.com; p83 devonduringww2;p85 Bill Brand; p85 www.ianvisits.co.uk; p87 Vick the Viking derivative work;p89 Navalhistory.net; p91 issuu.com; p97 ofshipssurgeons; p97 berkshirerecordoffice.org.uk; p105 21stCenturyGreenstuff : p105 U.S. National Archives and Records Administration; p107 Royal Burnham Yacht Club; p107 Justin Sutcliffe; p109 Maritime Quest; p111 ruslanguage; p115 Yousuf Karsh; p115 thehomefronthousewife; p119 National Gallery Canteen; p121 Ministry of Information; p123 SuperJet International; p127 Good Luck Symbols;

Whilst we have made every effort to contact copyright holders, should we have made any omission, please contact us so that we can make the appropriate acknowledgement.

CONTENTS

1943 HIGHLIGHTS

Monarch: King George VI   Prime Minister: Sir Winston Churchill — Conservative

In 1943, Winston Churchill's inspiring and resolute leadership was guiding the country through yet another year of rationing and austerity, virtually every household item was either in short supply and had to be queued for or was unobtainable. The blackout continued to cause widespread inconvenience; unnecessary travel was regarded as anti-social; Lord Woolton made a famous 'pie' and we were all asked to eat more potatoes and less bread.

News was of paramount importance and promulgated through the newspapers, the cinema and the radio. Half the nation would tune in to the nine o'clock news each evening.

But there was also a greater sense of optimism that the war was being won — and planning was beginning for the future. In 1943 the first of over 1.5 million American servicemen arrived on British shores to prepare for the Allied offensives and there was a feeling that after victory, the country could not go back to pre-war social conditions

Queuing for bread (above).
US Forces arrive (below).

FAMOUS PEOPLE WHO WERE BORN IN 1943

6th Jan: Terry Venables, Footballer & Manager
29th Jan: Tony Blackburn, DJ
25th Feb: George Harrison, Singer & Guitarist
9th Mar: Bobby Fischer, American Chess Player
5th May: Michael Palin, Comedian & Presenter
27th May: Cilla Black, Singer
17th June: Barry Manilow, Singer Songwriter
26th July: Mick Jagger, Rock Singer
18th Dec: Keith Richards, Rock Guitarist

FAMOUS PEOPLE WHO DIED IN 1943

7th Jan: Sir Henry Maybury, Civil Engineer
28th Mar: Sergei Rachmaninoff, Soviet Composer
3rd Apr: Conrad Veidt, German actor
30th Apr: Beatrice Webb, Socialist & Reformer
27th May: Arthur Mee, Topographer & Author
1st June: Leslie Howard, Actor
22nd Nov: Lorenzo Hart, American Composer
15th Dec: Fats Waller, American Jazz Pianist
22nd Dec: Beatrix Potter, English Author

OF THE YEAR

JANUARY   The Casablanca Conference. President Roosevelt, PM Winston Churchill and Generals Charles de Gaulle and Henri Giraud of the Free French Forces meet secretly to plan the Allied European strategy for the next stage of the war.

FEBRUARY   The Battle of Stalingrad comes to an end with the surrender of the German 6th Army.

MARCH   British prototype of the Mark I Colossus computer is constructed at Bletchley Park to help decode German signals.

APRIL   Easter Day occurs on 25th, the latest possible date in the Western Christian Church. The last time was in 1886 and the next will be 2038.

MAY   Operation Chastise, the Dambuster Raid, takes place when the RAF use bouncing bombs to breach German dams in the Ruhr Valley

JUNE   A scheduled passenger flight is shot down over the Bay of Biscay by German Junkers and all 17 persons aboard perish, including actor Leslie Howard.

JULY   'Il Duce', Benito Mussolini, Fascist Prime Minister of Italy, is arrested after the Grand Council of Fascism withdraws its support.

AUGUST   Louis Mountbatten is named Supreme Allied Commander for Southeast Asia.

SEPTEMBER   United States General Eisenhower publicly announces the surrender of Italy.

OCTOBER   The Burma Railway is completed between Bangkok in Thailand and Rangoon in Burma using the forced labour of Allied Prisoners of war.

NOVEMBER   Italy has joined the Allies at war against Germany and four bombs are dropped on the neutral Vatican City. The aircraft responsible is never certainly identified.

DECEMBER   The Regency Act is amended to allow Princess Elizabeth to become a Counsellor of State at age eighteen.

FILMS AND ARTS

The film **Casablanca**, an American romantic drama set during the present war and starring Humphrey Bogart and Ingrid Bergman is released nationally in the United States and becomes one of the top-grossing pictures.

Another war film, Noel Coward's production of **In Which We Serve** about the lives of the crew of a torpedoed and sinking destroyer during the battle of Crete and based on a true story, was nominated for two Oscars but failed to win.

For Whom the Bell Tolls an adaptation of Ernest Hemingway's romantic, adventure novel and **Heaven Can Wait**, a comedy film produced and directed by Ernst Lubitsch provided light relief.

When the war first broke out, the government closed the London theatres for fear that they would be hit by the bombings but gradually the rules were relaxed, they opened again and were an important escape from the problems of war.

Popular shows were **Blithe Spirit** by Noel Coward, **Hi-De-Hi** with Flanagan & Allen and **Lust for Love** starring and directed by John Gielgud.

The BBC played a huge part in the serious side of war but also brought entertainment with **Music While You Work** remaining one of the most popular programmes with **Desert Island Discs** and the first adaptation of **The Railway Children.**

1943 THE YEAR

Born in 1943, you were one of 48.25 million people living in Britain and your life expectancy *then* was about 63 years. You were one of the 16.1 births per 1,000 population and you had a 3.1% (the lowest rate yet recorded) chance of dying as an infant, most likely from an infectious disease such as polio, diphtheria, tetanus, whooping cough, measles, mumps or rubella.

The country was living under unprecedented regulations governing every aspect of life, no-one in your family would be 'untouched' by the war and you would be reliant on rationing and ration books for some years to come. But, you were at the beginning of the end of the war, the country was planning for the future and the future was to turn the old 'social order' upside down.

Paper was severely rationed and 'The Times' and 'Daily Mirror' both ran to only 8 pages. News was often delayed for reporting – for example, details of storm damage or new machinery - to prevent information 'helping' the enemy.

In 1943, the standard rate of income tax was in excess of 40%, a higher rate was charged on incomes over £2,000 and saving was encouraged. The country needed money to fight the war. Clothes were rationed but when not 'making do and mend', the government had intervened in the mass manufacture of high street fashions with the arrival of the purchase tax free, 'utility' clothing scheme. Accommodation in cities was often scarce, unscrupulous landlords raised rents, and agricultural workers were provided with Government cottages. Cheap 'utility' furniture was made; central heating was unheard of, coal fires heated houses – and coal was rationed. When you heard the air raid siren you might go to the Anderson shelter in the garden; children helped with the harvest; cinemas thrived for entertainment and newsreels and by 1943 more than 1,300 pubs had closed due to enemy action but 'the local' was still a comforting place to go to - and everybody seemed to smoke!

WAR TIME BASIC RATIONS

On *average*, one adult weekly ration:
Bacon and ham – 4oz (110gms)
1s 10d (9p) worth of meat – about 8oz
2oz (50gms) butter -
2oz cheese
4oz margarine
3 pts of milk
8oz (230gms) of sugar
2oz tea leaves
1 Egg

YOU WERE BORN

POPULAR CULTURE

Vera Lynn was known as 'the Forces sweetheart' and her iconic songs of the war years included **There'll Be Blue Birds Over** and **A Nightingale Sang in Berkeley Square.** In America much of the music was from the Big Bands, jazz or swing. **That Old Black Magic** by Glenn Miller and the sentimental **You'll Never Know** by Dick Haymes were hits in Britain too.

Vera Lynn sings to the troops.

Noël Coward's satirical song, **Don't Let's Be Beastly to The Germans** which, although popular when performed live and allegedly Winston Churchill demanded an encore when he first heard it, caused controversy on the wireless and the BBC banned it.

The London revival of **Show Boat** by Jerome Kern and Oscar Hammerstein had a lengthy run at the Stoll Theatre in London and Vera Lynn starred in **We'll Meet Again**, the musical film set during the Blitz and loosely based on the star's life.

In January, Winston Churchill attended the Casablanca Conference and found time to paint a view of the Kutubiyya Mosque in Marrakesh, which he then presented to President Roosevelt.

The children's book, **The Little Prince** by the exiled French aviator Antoine de Saint-Exupéry was published and becomes a best seller and Arthur Ransome published **The Picts and the Martyrs,** his eleventh and last book in the **Swallows and Amazons** series set in the Lake District.

Colossus, the world's first electronic computer, developed at Bletchley Park, had a single purpose: to help decipher the Lorenz-encrypted (Tunny) messages between Hitler and his generals.

WARTIME SPORT

At the beginning of the war, football was suspended 'until official notice to the contrary'. The threat of air attack and the introduction of conscription made it impossible for the game to continue as before. However, by September 1939, the rules relaxed to allow a revised programme of football if it 'didn't interfere with national service and industry'. There was a limited regional league and cup programme. Inter-service matches took place and football remained a popular spectator sport.

Education between the ages of 5 and 15 was made compulsory in 1944. In 1948, there were no state preschools or nurseries and all children who had now returned to their family having been evacuated from the towns and cities for the duration of the war, together with children who had stayed at home, would be setting off for school for the first time. It could be a very tearful day for both mother and child! But for the child, school life had a routine – calling the register, lessons, playtime and at mid-morning, a third-of-a-pint bottle of milk.

Reading, writing and arithmetic were most important; times tables were learnt by rote as was poetry; neat handwriting was practised daily, and nature study was 'science' when leaves and acorns were identified and then later become 'arts and crafts'.

Children At Five

Five in 1948, sweets were still rationed and Mothers would gather the coupons together for the children and they could choose sweeties from the rows of jars on the shelves. Blackjacks, barley sugar twists, sherbet Dabs, dolly mixture or toffees. Two of the first new sweets to be introduced after the war, in 1948, were Spangles and Polos. You could laugh at the antics in the Beano and Dandy comics and play with toy guns and soldiers, wheel your dolly in her pram, race your Dinky toy cars or have a doll's tea party in your 'pretend' house.

How Much Did It Cost?

The Average Pay:	£325	(£6 7s p.w)
The Average House:	£900	
Loaf of White Bread:	4d (2p)	
Pint of Milk:	4½d (2p)	
Pint of Beer:	1s (15p)	
Gallon of Petrol:	5s (25p)	
12mths Road Tax	£10	
Newspapers:	1d - 3d (1p)	
To post a letter in UK:	2½d (1p)	
TV Licence B/White	£2 + £1 for radio	

YOU WERE FIVE

POPULAR CULTURE

Dorothy Squires was 'top of the pops' in 1948, her hit song **A Tree in the Meadow** was rated No1 by the number of copies of sheet music sold. From America, Dinah Shore and her Happy Valley Boys, made a splash with **Buttons and Bows**.

The first Aldeburgh Festival founded by Benjamin Britten and Peter Pears was held in June.

The first volume of Winston Churchill's **The Second World War** was published

The film of Shakespeare's **Hamlet,** adapted, directed and starring Sir Laurence Olivier was shown and goes on to win the Oscar for Best Picture.

The Red Shoes the British film starring Moira Shearer was the debut of the ballerina as an actress and the majority of the cast were also professional dancers. The film received a total of five Academy Award nominations and was a major financial success.

London theatre had its best business for 10 years in 1948 with **Kiss Me Kate** being just one of many popular musicals.

The BBC had shown cinema newsreels since 1936, but as interest in TV grew, the demand for a dedicated news service increased. Introduced by famous commentator John Snagge, **BBC Newsreel** showed filmed short reports of the day's events.

Children could be entertained by the BBC's new children's television service with one of its earliest successes, **Muffin the Mule,** a loveable puppet whose antics were accompanied on the piano by Annette Mills.

Approximately 100,000 UK households had a television in 1948 and 68.5 hours of The London Olympic Games was shown live. It was the most ambitious sustained outside broadcast yet attempted by the BBC and was completed without serious problems.

1954 THE YEAR

AFTER THE WAR
THE 'NEW LOOK'

As the decade began, the simple, drab, styles from wartime remained as materials were still in short supply and for many this remained the case for several years. However, with the introduction of colour into the country again, in the home and in textiles, fashion for many women returned with a vengeance. The years are known for two silhouettes, that of Christian Dior's 'New Look', the tiny waist, pointy breasts and a full skirt to just below the knee, all achieved with a "waspie" girdle and the pointiest bra seen in history and the pencil slim tubular skirt, also placing emphasis on a narrow waist.

Neat, tailored suits with pencil skirts or fitted dresses, now updated with block colours were the choice for work and by the second half of the decade, the wide circle skirts in colourful cotton prints were in and were worn supported by bouffant net petticoats, stiffened either with conventional starch or a strong sugar solution, to give the right look.

THE *Lift* THAT NEVER LETS YOU DOWN

Britain was almost obsessed with all things American after the war and the first Wimpy Bars opened in Britain in 1954, selling hamburgers, expresso coffee and milkshakes. Named after a fat friend of 'Popeye', the Wimpy bar added the 'British' elements of waitress service and cutlery. They became very popular, especially with the decade's 'new' teenagers who welcomed the addition to the high street's coffee bars and juke boxes.

ELEVEN IN 1954

Age eleven was a milestone year for children. They went from being the 'king-pins' at primary school to 'the newcomers', either at Grammar School if they'd passed the 11+ exam or Secondary Modern if not.

It was the start of growing up but at home there was still plenty of fun. Streets had little traffic and could be transformed with a couple of pullovers into a football or cricket pitch. Girls could spend hours skipping or playing hopscotch drawn on the path, whilst their 'babies' slept in toy prams.

HOW MUCH DID IT COST?

The Average Pay:	£500 (£9 9s p.w)
The Average House:	£1860
Loaf of White Bread:	7½d (3p)
Pint of Milk:	7d (3p)
Pint of Beer:	1s 6d (7p)
12mnths Road Tax	£12 10s (£12.50)
Gallon of Petrol:	4s 6d (5p/litre)
Newspapers:	5d - 1s (2p)
To post a letter in UK:	2½d (1p)
TV Licence	£3 Black & White + £1 radio

YOU WERE ELEVEN

POPULAR CULTURE

The best-selling record of the year was **Secret Love** sung by the actress Doris Day in the film **Calamity Jane.** Other hits included **Blowing Wild** by Frankie Lane; the trumpet of Eddie Calvert with **Oh Mein Papa** and a surprise hit for the comedian Norman Wisdom with **Don't Laugh at Me 'Cos I'm a Fool.**

In January the tall, handsome baseball hero, captured the heart of the beautiful, glamorous Hollywood star and Marilyn Monroe and Joe DiMaggio were married.

JRR Tolkien published the first of his **Lord of the Rings** trilogy, **The Fellowship of the Ring**, and William Golding, his morality tale, **Lord of the Flies.**

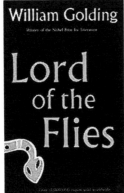

From Here to Eternity won the cinema accolades but there were other successful films this year including, **White Christmas** with Bing Crosby, **The Caine Mutiny** starring Humphrey Bogart and Kirk Douglas in **20,000 Leagues Under the Sea.**

The art exhibitions at the **Venice Biennale** are revived, introducing American abstract expressionism to Europe.

Two months after the author's death, Richard Burton made famous his 'First Voice' in Dylan Thomas's radio play, **Under Milk Wood.**

"I'm in a ticklish position here!"

The buxom young women, fat old ladies, drunken men, honeymoon couples and vicars of Donald McGill, the artist of the 'saucy seaside postcard', led him to a £50 for breaching the Obscene Publications Act.

George Cowling gave BBC's first televised live and 'in vision' weather forecast He stood in front of the weather map, using a pencil and rubber to show the weather for the next day and informed the viewers that *'tomorrow would be rather windy, a good day to hang out the washing'.*

A FRIENDLY WASH-DAY WARNING —ON TV

1958 THE YEAR

The fifties were a decade of rapid economic growth and in 1958, the country's reserves of coal were sufficient for domestic rationing to end. Towns and cities were being reshaped by a massive building programme of council estates, tower blocks and shopping centres.

1958: In June, the first parking meter in Britain was installed in Grosvenor Square, near the US Embassy in Westminster. Parking for one hour cost six shillings (30p) and those who overstayed or neglected to pay at all received a £2 penalty.

It was the year Donald Campbell broke the water speed record; the tragedy of the Manchester United football team's air crash; the Queen officially reopened Gatwick Airport; the first Duke of Edinburgh Award was presented; debutantes were no longer presented at court; **Grandstand** and **Blue Peter** both made their debut on BBC television and **Bridge on the River Kwai** was a huge success.

LIFE AT FIFTEEN

Fifteen in 1958, you were now old enough to leave school and venture into the world of work, but not the armed forces; you still had to wait a year to legally buy cigarettes – and smoke them and you couldn't buy a beer in a pub. The consumer boom had arrived with 'teen' clothes becoming available and fashion was influenced by America. Rock 'n' roll and film stars set fashions. There were the Teddy Boys and Beatniks.

HOW MUCH DID IT COST?

The Average Pay:	£650 (£12 p.w)
The Average House:	£2,100
Loaf of White Bread:	11d (5p)
Pint of Milk:	8d (3p
Pint of Beer:	2s (10p)
Gallon of Petrol:	(5s 8p) (8p/litre)
12mnths Road Tax	£12 10s (£12.50)
Newspapers:	43p - 8p
To post a letter in UK:	3d (1p)
TV Licence	£4 Black & White

YOU WERE 15

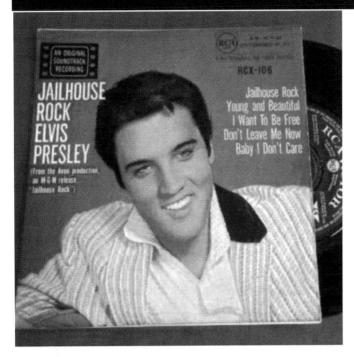

POPULAR MUSIC

Elvis Presley had the most top 10 entries in 1958, with five, and all of them peaking within the top three. In January, **Jailhouse Rock** became the first-ever record to debut at No1 in the UK and went on to become the year's best-selling single.

The 1957 Christmas No1, **Mary's Boy Child** by Harry Belafonte stayed at No1 for two weeks in January.

JANUARY **Great Balls of Fire** was the first new No1 of the year for Jerry Lee Lewis.

FEBRUARY Pat Boone took **April Love** to No 7 in the charts. Written as the theme song for the film of the same name, starring Pat Boone, it was nominated for an Oscar for Best Music but lost out to **All the Way** by Frank Sinatra.

JUNE The Everly Brothers had three top 10 entries including **All I Have to Do is Dream** which spent seven weeks at No 1.

JULY Marty Wilde had his first chart hit with **Endless Sleep** a teenage 'tragedy' song, a hit in the US by Jody Reynolds, but originally thought by record companies as 'too depressing'.

OCTOBER Cliff Richard had a hit **Move It**, backed by The Drifters who later changed their name to The Shadows.

DECEMBER **It's Only Make Believe** peaked at No 1 on Christmas Day and Conway Twitty stayed at the top for five weeks.

Doctors and scientists were beginning to gather evidence of the link between smoking and lung cancer and that it was harmful to your health, but in 1958 it was still promoted as a 'healthy', 'social' and 'fun' activity.

1964 THE YEAR

In 1964 Britain was engulfed in Beatlemania; mini-skirts were on the rise; Mods and Rockers took to fighting at the seaside and it was the year of The Great Train Robbery.

In October, thirteen years of Tory rule ended when Harold Wilson was elected Labour Prime Minister and in America, anti-Vietnam war protests were increasing.

The Forth Road Bridge opened; Winston Churchill retired and Radio Caroline, the 'pirate radio station' began broadcasting from a ship just outside UK territorial waters off Suffolk.

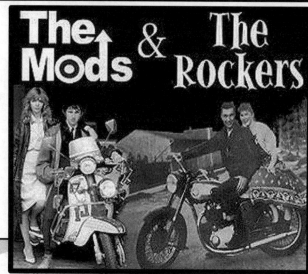

BUTLIN'S HOLIDAY CAMP SKEGNESS
IT'S QUICKER BY RAIL

Your holiday was still likely to be taken in England.

Holiday camps such as Butlins with their 'Red Coats' offered hours of fun, coaches could take you to the seaside and owning a caravan was becoming popular too. If you ate out, fish and chips was the most usual but Chinese restaurants were on the increase and teenagers loved the 'Wimpey Bar' for burgers.

THE FORTH ROAD BRIDGE

In September, the longest suspension bridge in the world outside America at this time, the Forth Road Bridge, opened spanning the Firth of Forth connecting Edinburgh to Fife. It has a main span of 1,100 yards between the two towers and in total, the structure is over 1.5 miles long. The diameter of the main cable is 1' 11¼" and the total length of wire in the main cables is 30,800 miles. 39,000 tons of steel and 164,000 cubic yards of concrete was used in its construction.

HOW MUCH DID IT COST?

The Average Pay:	£915 (£18 p.w)
The Average House:	£3,092
Loaf of White Bread:	1s 2d (6p)
Pint of Milk:	9d (4p)
Pint of Beer:	2s 3d (11p)
Gallon of Petrol:	5s 1p (25p)
12mnths Road Tax	£15
Newspapers:	3d - 9d (1p - 3)p
To post a letter in UK:	3d (1p)
TV Licence	£5 Black & White

POPULAR CULTURE

For the second successive year, The Beatles had the biggest-selling single of the year with **Can't Buy Me Love**. It spent three weeks at No1.

The group had a total of five top 10 entries, including two No1's from 1963, **She Loves You** and **I Want to Hold Your Hand** plus their fifth and sixth No1's **A Hard Day's Night** and **I Feel Fine**.

JANUARY **Glad All Over** by the Dave Clark Five was their first No1 hit and knocked the Beatles **I Want to Hold Your Hand** off the top spot.

FEBRUARY Bacharach and David wrote **Anyone Who Had a Heart** for Dionne Warwick but her version lost out to Cilla Black's in the UK, which stayed at No1 for three weeks

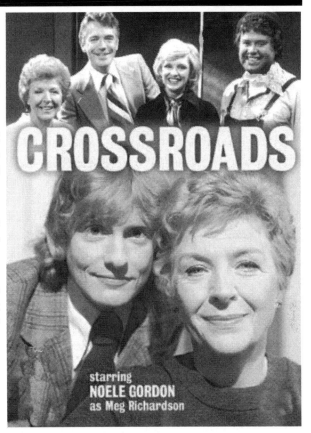

starring
NOELE GORDON
as Meg Richardson

The daily soap opera **Crossroads** began in 1964. Set in a fictional motel in the Midlands the programme became the byword for cheap production values and had huge negative criticism – but despite this, it was loved by millions of regular fans.

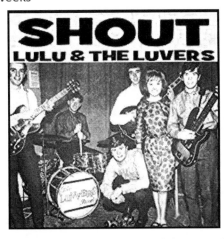

JUNE Scottish singer Lulu has her debut No1 hit with the Isley Brothers' 1959 hit, **Shout**.

JULY **A Hard Day's Night** by the Beatles featured on the soundtrack of their first feature film. The song topped the charts in both the UK and US.

OCTOBER Bare foot Sandie Shaw had her first No1 with **Always Something There to Remind Me**. Written by Bacharach and David, it had previously been 'demoed' by Dionne Warwick.

NOVEMBER **Little Red Rooster** by The Rolling Stones became the first blues standard to reach No1 but within a week Gene Pitney took the top spot with **I'm Gonna be Strong**.

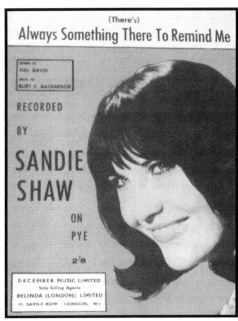

1943 THE WAR

January

27th 50 bombers mount the first all American air raid against Germany. Wilhelmshaven, the large naval base, is the primary target.

February

11th U.S. General Dwight D. Eisenhower is selected to command the Allied armies in Europe.

March

5th : Essen is bombed, marking the beginning of a four-month attack on the Ruhr industrial area.

13th German forces liquidate the Jewish ghetto in Kraków.

17th Devastating convoy losses in the Atlantic due to increased U-boat activity.

April

19th The Warsaw Ghetto uprising: On the Eve of Passover, Jews resist German attempts to deport the Jewish community.

28th : Allies attempt to close the mid-Atlantic gap in the war against the U-boats with long-range bombers.

May

15th The French form a "Resistance Movement".

16th The Warsaw Ghetto Uprising ends. The ghetto has been destroyed, with about 14,000 Jews killed and 40,000 sent to the death camps at Majdanek and Treblinka.

16th The Dambuster Raids are carried out by RAF 617 Squadron on two German dams, Mohne and Eder. The Ruhr war industries lose electrical power.

24th Admiral Karl Dönitz orders the majority of U-boats to withdraw from the Atlantic because of heavy losses to new Allied anti-submarine tactics.

29th RAF bombs Wuppertal, causing heavy civilian losses.

July

7th Walter Dornberger briefs the V-2 rocket to Hitler, who approves the project for top priority.

24th Hamburg, Germany, is heavily bombed in Operation Gomorrah, which at the time is the heaviest assault in the history of aviation.

August

29th During the Occupation of Denmark by Nazi Germany, martial law replaced the Danish government.

September

3rd Nazi Germany begins the evacuation of civilians from Berlin.

22nd British midget submarines attack the German battleship Tirpitz, at anchor in a Norwegian fjord, crippling her for six months.

30th Danes are secretly sending their Jewish countrymen to Sweden by boat crossings.

October

4th Corsica is liberated by Free French forces.

19th The German War Office contracts the Mittelwerk to produce 12,000 V-2 rockets.

22/23rd An air raid on Kassel causes a seven-day firestorm.

November

9th General De Gaulle becomes President of the French Committee of National Liberation.

27th Huge civilian losses in Berlin as heavy bombing raids continue.

December

14th United States XV Corps arrives in European Theatre.

24th US General Dwight D. Eisenhower becomes the Supreme Allied Commander in Europe.

26th German battleship *Scharnhorst* is sunk off North Cape (in the Arctic) by a British force led by the battleship HMS *Duke of York*.

27th General Eisenhower is officially named head of Overlord, the invasion of Normandy.

SUMMARY

1943 saw Germany in control of continental Europe, occupying from France in the west, to Italy in the south and east to Russia. However the tide was starting to turn with greater resistance from occupied people and increasingly heavy Allied bombing raids over German cities and industrial areas.

The RAF Dambusters

The British Air Ministry had identified the industrialised Ruhr Valley, especially its dams, as important strategic targets. The dams provided hydroelectric power and pure water for steel-making, drinking water and water for the canal transport system. A one-off surprise attack might succeed but the RAF lacked a weapon suitable for the task. The mission grew out of a concept for a large barrel shaped bomb designed by Barnes Wallis. The bomb would skip across the surface of the water before hitting the dam wall and then run down the side of the dam towards its base, thus maximising the explosive effect against the dam.

The targets selected were the Möhne Dam and the Sorpe Dam, upstream from the Ruhr industrial area, with the Eder Dam on the Eder River as a secondary target.

On the night of 6/17 May, 19 Lancaster bombers took off flying at a very low altitude, just above wave height to avoid detection. One struck the sea, one an electricity pylon and one was shot down over Holland. Five bombers reached the Möhne dam and four dropped their bombs with the last breaching the dam wall.
Three bombers reached the Eder dam and they successfully breached the dam. The attacks on the Sorpe and Ennepe Dams were unsuccessful. On the way back, flying again at treetop level, two more Lancasters were lost meaning only eleven out of the original eighteen survived.

The Möhne and Edersee dams were breached, causing catastrophic flooding of the Ruhr valley Two hydroelectric power stations were destroyed . Factories and mines were also damaged and destroyed. An estimated 1,600 civilians – about 600 Germans and 1,000 forced labourers, mainly Soviet – were killed by the flooding. Despite rapid repairs by the Germans, production did not return to normal until September. The RAF lost 53 aircrew killed and 3 captured, with 8 aircraft destroyed.

1943 THE WAR

January

10th Soviet troops launch an all-out offensive attack on Stalingrad

21st The last airfield at Stalingrad is taken by Red Army forces, ensuring that the Luftwaffe will be unable to supply German troops any further.

24th German forces in Stalingrad are in the last phases of collapse.

February

2nd The Soviet Union, the Battle of Stalingrad comes to an end with the official surrender of the German 6th Army.

March

13th German forces liquidate the Jewish ghetto in Kraków.

14th Germans recapture Kharkov.

16th The first reports of the Katyn massacre in Poland seep to the West; reports say that more than 22,000 prisoners of war were killed by the NKVD (Russian Political Police), who eventually blame the massacre on the Germans.

April

15th Finland officially rejects Soviet terms for peace.

July

12th The Battle of Prokhorovka begins the largest tank battle in human history and part of the Battle of Kursk, it is the pivotal battle of Operation Citadel.

13th Hitler calls off the Kursk offensive, but the Soviets continue the battle.

August

5th Swedish government announces it will no longer allow German troops and war material to transit Swedish railways.

5th Russians recapture Orel and Belgorod.

23rd Operation Polkovodets Rumyantsev liberates Kharkov, Ukraine. The Battle of Kursk has become the first successful major

Belongings abandoned as Jews are cleared from Krakow

September

4th Soviet Union declares war on Bulgaria.

25th The Red Army retakes Smolensk.

November

6th The Red Army liberates the city of Kiev. This is an anniversary of the Russian Revolution in 1917.

16th Kalinin is retaken in a large Red Army offensive.

26th The Red Army offensive in the Ukraine continues.

Stalin, Roosevelt and Churchill meet to discuss war strategy.

SUMMARY

1943 sees the Russian Red army inflict successive heavy losses on the German army. Stalingrad is regained, cutting off supplies to the German troops who are pushed back west. Russia start to occupy the Ukraine and some Baltic states and advance in Bulgaria.
For the first time, Germany is in retreat.

THE BATTLE FOR STALINGRAD

The Germans had reached Stalingrad in August 1942. By October 1942 90% of Stalingrad was destroyed, and all civilians were manning the defences. The Germans has almost complete control but in November much of the German air force was sent away to help in North Africa and the freezing weather caught the Germans unprepared and ill-equipped. The Russians started to counter attack and surrounded the German force.

The Germans tried to evacuate their troops and by 18 December were only 30ml from Stalingrad but were ordered back. The military and political leadership of Nazi Germany sought not to relieve them, but to get them to fight on for as long as possible so as to tie up the Soviet forces.

The Red Army offered the Germans a chance to surrender on 7 January 1943. If they surrendered within 24 hours, there would be a guarantee of safety for all prisoners, medical care for the sick and wounded, prisoners being allowed to keep their personal belongings, "normal" food rations, and repatriation to any country they wished after the war. Hitler rejected this offer.

The Germans were now not only starving but running out of ammunition. Nevertheless, they continued to resist, in part because they believed the Soviets would execute any who surrendered.

On 22 January, Russia once again offered Paulus, the German commander, a chance to surrender. He told Hitler that he was no longer able to command his men, who were without ammunition or food. Hitler rejected this surrender on a point of honour. On 31st January 1943, the 10th anniversary of Hitler's coming to power Soviet forces reached the entrance to the German headquarters. Around 91,000 exhausted, ill, wounded, and starving prisoners were taken. The prisoners included 22 generals. The battle was over. On 2nd February.

The Axis suffered 747,300 – 868,374 combat casualties (killed, wounded or captured) among all branches of the German armed forces and their allies. The Germans lost 900 aircraft, 500 tanks and 6,000 artillery pieces. The USSR, suffered 1,129,619 total casualties; 478,741 personnel killed or missing, and 650,878 wounded or sick. The USSR lost 4,341 tanks destroyed or damaged, 15,728 artillery pieces and 2,769 combat aircraft.

1943 THE WAR IN AFRICA

January
15th The British start an offensive aimed at taking Tripoli, Libya.
23th British capture Tripoli, Libya

February
2nd Rommel retreats farther into Tunisia. Within two days, Allied troops move into Tunisia for the first time.
5th The Allies now have all of Libya under their control.
8th : United States' VI Corps arrives in North Africa.
13th Rommel launches a counter-attack against the Americans in western Tunisia; he takes Sidi Bouzid and Gafsa. The Battle of the Kasserine Pass begins: inexperienced American troops are soon forced to retreat.

March
6th Battle of Medenine, Tunisia. It is Rommel's last battle in Africa as he is forced to retreat.
18th General George S. Patton leads his tanks of II Corps into Gafsa, Tunisia.
20th Montgomery's forces begin a breakthrough in Tunisia, striking at the Mareth line.
23th American tanks defeat the Germans at El Guettar, Tunisia.
26th The British break through the Mareth line in southern Tunisia, threatening the whole German army. The Germans move north.

April
7th Hitler and Mussolini come together at Salzburg, mostly for the purpose of propping up Mussolini's fading morale.
Allied forces–the Americans from the West, the British from the East–link up near Gafsa in Tunisia.

May
7th Tunis captured by British First Army. Meanwhile, the Americans take Bizerte.
13th Remaining German Afrika Korps and Italian troops in North Africa surrender to Allied forces. The Allies take over 250,000 prisoners
22nd Allies bomb Sicily and Sardinia, both possible landing sites.
31st American B-17's bomb Naples.

June
11th British 1st Division takes the Italian island of Pantelleria, between Tunisia and Sicily, capturing 11,000 Italian troops.
12th The Italian island of Lampedusa, between Tunisia and Sicily, surrenders to the Allies.

July
10th The Allied invasion of Sicily begins.
19th The Allies bomb Rome for the first time
22nd U.S. forces under Patton capture Palermo, Sicily

August
6th German troops start to take over Italy's defences.
11th German and Italian forces begin to evacuate Sicily.
17th All of Sicily now controlled by the Allies.

September
3rd A secret Italian Armistice is signed and Italy drops out of the war. Mainland Italy is invaded when the British XXIII Corps lands at Reggio Calabria.
8th Eisenhower publicly announces the surrender of Italy to the Allies.
9th The Allies land at Salerno, Italy.
10th German troops occupy Rome. The Italian fleet surrenders at Malta and other Mediterranean ports.
28th The people of Naples, sensing the approach of the Allies, rise up against the German occupiers.

October
1st Neapolitans complete their uprising and free Naples from German military occupation.
13th Italy declares war on Germany.

November
5th The Vatican is bombed in a failed attempt to knock out the Vatican radio.

SUMMARY
1943 saw strong Allied gains in all regions. By May, the Allies had captured N. Africa and over 250,000 prisoners. The campaign to free Italy started and soon had taken Sicily with the Italians on the run, so much so that Hitler sent his own troops in to fight instead of the Italians. Italy eventually declared war on Germany!

Montgomery talks to British troops near Catania

British troops scramble over a devastated street in Catania, Sicily, 5 August 1943.

ALLIES CAPTURE SICILY

Sicily was defended by 200,000 Italian troops, 70,000 German troops and 30,000 *Luftwaffe* ground staff. The German commanders in Sicily were contemptuous of their allies and German units took their orders from Generalfeldmarschall Albert Kesselring.

The night of 9–10 July, just south of Syracuse, was the start of the joint American and British invasion. Strong winds blew 69 gliders off course, crashing into the sea, with over 200 men drowning. Landings were made the same night on 26 main beaches of the southern and eastern coasts of the island . This was the largest amphibious operation of World War II. The Italian defensive plan did not contemplate large beach landings so the Allies encountered no major resistance.

By 27 July, the Axis commanders had realised that the Italians and Germans would retreat to the Italian mainland through the port of Messina. Organised by the Germans the full-scale withdrawal began on 11 August and continued to 17 August. The Germans made successive withdrawals each night of between 8 and 24 kilometres (5 and 15 miles), keeping the following Allied units at arm's length with the use of mines, demolitions and other obstacles and despite the Allies attempting to counter this the evacuation proved highly successful.

The Italians evacuated 62,182 men, 41 guns and 227 vehicles. The Germans evacuated some 52,000 troops. The Allies had taken Sicily in a month with over 22,000 casualties (5,700 killed or missing, 16,000 wounded, and 3,300 captured), while the Germans lost 8,900 men killed or missing, 5,532 captured and 13,500 wounded, with Italian military losses of 40,700 killed or missing, 32,500 wounded and 116,681 captured.

1943 THE WAR

January

2nd Americans and Australians recapture Buna, New Guinea.

February

8th The Chindits (a "long range penetration group") under British General Orde Wingate begin an incursion into Burma.

9th Guadalcanal is finally secured; it is the first major victory of the American offensive in the Pacific war.

18th Chindits under Wingate cut the railway line between Mandalay and Myitkyina.

21st Americans take the Russell Islands, part of the Solomons chain.

April

4th The only large-scale escape of Allied prisoners-of-war from the Japanese in the Pacific takes place when ten American POWs and two Filipino convicts break out of the Davao Penal Colony on the island of Mindanao in the southern Philippines. The escaped POWs were the first to break the news of the infamous Bataan Death March and other atrocities committed by the Japanese, to the world.

May

2nd Japanese aircraft again bomb Darwin, Australia.

11th American and Canadian troops invade Attu Island in the Aleutian Islands in an attempt to expel occupying Japanese forces.

30th Attu Island is again under American control.

June

8th Japanese forces begin to evacuate Kiska Island in the Aleutians, their last foothold in the West.

21st American troops land in the Trobriand Islands, close to New Guinea. The American strategy of driving up the Southwest Pacific by "Island Hopping" continues.

22nd The Cairo Conference: US President Franklin D. Roosevelt, British Prime Minister Winston Churchill, and ROC leader Chiang Kai-shek meet in Cairo, Egypt, to discuss ways to defeat Japan.

25th Rangoon is bombed by American heavy bombers.

July

6th U.S. and Japanese ships fight the Battle of Kula Gulf in the Solomons.

August

6th Japan declares independence for the State of Burma under Dr. Ba Maw.

6/7th The U.S. wins the Battle of Vella in the Solomons.

September

21st The battle of the Solomons can now be considered at an unofficial end.

22nd Australian forces land at Finschhafen, a small port in New Guinea. The Japanese continue the battle well into October.

October

3rd Churchill appoints Lord Louis Mountbatten the commander of South East Asia Command.

7th The Japanese execute 98 American civilians on Wake Island.

November

1st In Operation Goodtime, United States Marines land on Bougainville in the Solomon Islands. The fighting on this island will continue to the end of the war.

20: US Marines land on Tarawa and the American public is shocked by the heavy losses suffered by their forces.

December

29th Control of the Andaman Islands is handed over to Azad Hind by the Japanese.

SUMMARY

1943 saw the Allied forces slowly gain naval and air supremacy in the Pacific. They moved methodically from island to island, conquering them one at a time despite sustaining significant casualties.

The Japanese, however, successfully defended their positions on the Chinese mainland and much of SE Asia until 1945.

IN ASIA AND THE PACIFIC

Japanese school girls wave off a Kamikaze pilot (top).

American aircraft carrier USS Bunker Hill burns after being hit by two kamikaze planes (Bottom right).

US Marines advancing (Bottom left)

THE ISLAND HOPPING STRATEGY

Leapfrogging, also known as island hopping, was a military strategy employed by the Allies in the Pacific War against the Empire of Japan during World War II. The key idea is to bypass heavily fortified enemy islands instead of trying to capture every island in sequence en route to a final target. The reasoning is that those islands can simply be cut off from their supply chains (leading to their eventual capitulation) rather than needing to be overwhelmed by superior force, thus speeding up progress and reducing losses of troops and material. This would allow the United States forces to reach Japan quickly and not expend the time, manpower, and supplies to capture every Japanese-held island on the way. It would give the Allies the advantage of surprise and keep the Japanese off balance.

This strategy was possible in part because the Allies used submarine and air attacks to blockade and isolate Japanese bases, weakening their garrisons and reducing the Japanese ability to resupply and reinforce them. Thus troops on islands which had been bypassed, such as the major base at Rabaul, were useless to the Japanese war effort and left to "wither on the vine". This strategy began to be implemented in late 1943 in Operation Cartwheel. MacArthur's Operation Cartwheel, Operation Reckless and Operation Persecution were the first successful Allied practices of leapfrogging in terms of landing on lightly guarded beaches and very low casualties but cutting off Japanese troops hundreds of miles away from their supply routes.

JANUARY 1ST - 7TH 1943

IN THE NEWS

Friday 1 "New Year Pageant" Representatives of all the armed services attended the Royal Albert Hall. Flags of the 'Empire and Her Allies' were paraded and held high as the auditorium stood and sang 'Abide with Me'.

Saturday 2 "Drive to Double Girl's Army" Women's Land Army officials want 50,000 new recruits. Employment Exchanges are recruiting more women for daily work on our farms.

Sunday 3 "War Production in America" A mission from the Ministry of Aircraft Production has arrived in Washington from London to confer on the coordination of British and American technical practices and design.

Monday 4 "Health is Better Despite War" The Minister of Health confirmed to American medical observers that, in the fourth year of the war, our nation's health is better than in peacetime.

Tuesday 5 "Temporary Officers Insured" Commissioned offers will now be made eligible for the unemployment insurance scheme whereby on demob, should they become unemployed, they will be eligible for benefits alongside other ranks.

Wednesday 6 "More Food Restrictions" In order that as much shipping as possible may be used for military operations and the carriage of military supplies, the supply and consumption of food will be scaled down still further in the first six months of this new year.

Thursday 7 "Ship's Steward Wins BEM as 'Surgeon'" A chief steward in the Merchant Navy has been awarded the BEM for performing surgery on a torn kneecap of a crew member while his ship, on an Atlantic convoy, was being incessantly bombed by enemy planes.

HERE IN BRITAIN
"Furniture for New Homes"

Only utility furniture will be made in the future, and it will not be available for the public at large but rationed among certain priority classes. Maximum prices (lower than they would otherwise have been because the furniture is free of purchase tax) have been fixed, and the arrangements made for distribution come into force this week. The furniture, except nursery furniture, will be obtainable on surrender of a buying permit, which will be issued only to those setting up a home on marriage or in anticipation of the birth of a child and to those who have lost a home by bombing.

AROUND THE WORLD
"Absent on New Year's Day"

Over a hundred ringleaders, in advance of hundreds more men, were charged in Sydney with taking the day off on January 1st without 'reasonable cause' and in contravention of the National Security Regulations which had made December 28th a holiday instead. There had been no official union protests when the rules changed three months ago, but more recently, some workers protested that they were entitled to the holiday on December 28th in lieu of Boxing Day which fell on a Saturday – and therefore they should be paid extra rates on New Year's Day. When this demand was refused the men took the day off anyway.

HONOURS FOR THE LADIES

The WAAF (member of the Women's Auxiliary Air Force) who designed the large map on which the counters, denoting RAF and enemy planes, were plotted during the Battle of Britain, is to be honoured by the King. Sergeant Edith Mosscrop made a subsequent map for the operations of No 11 Group Fighter Command and it was on this map that the swarms of fighters put in the air during the Dieppe raid were directed. Employed before the war by London County Council as a planner of parks and recreation grounds, she was mentioned twice in dispatches for her work at No 11 Group headquarters. Sergeant Mosscrop will receive the British Empire Medal and she is just one of the women serving with the forces named in the New Years' Honours List.

Sergeant Florence May has already served in the Women's Air Force during the first world war and afterwards had settled down to run a laundry near Maidstone. This time round she has won the BEM for her devotion to duty in camp messes during intensive enemy air attacks and in Edinburgh, Mrs Marjorie Plain, back in civvy street, was previously a corporal in the Auxiliary Territorial Service (ATS) and her cooking has won her award.

Former cinema box office girl, Private Millicent Richardson, took up the dangerous job of a gun-site girl. Her work on the 'predictor' has won her a medal. The Sperry Predictor is a large black box, covered in dials, knobs and levers, operated by six 'Ack-Ack' girls and used to calculate the length of fuse needed to ensure the gunners shells explode at the right moment. With steady nerves under gunfire, they track the enemy aircraft crossing the sky, calculate the length of fuse and shout the information to the gunners.

JANUARY 8ᵀᴴ - 14ᵀᴴ 1943

IN THE NEWS

Friday 8 — **"Machines for the Farms"** An appeal was made to all farmers to purchase only essential agricultural machinery and tools to preserve the steel so as to equip our armies.

Saturday 9 — **"Shell Eggs in the Shops Again"** The first allocation of 1943 has begun, and the Ministry of Food confidently expects that by the end of the month, priority consumers will have had 12 eggs and other people one each.

Sunday 10 — **"American Sardines on the Way"** Twenty million tins of American and Canadian sardines will be released for sale at 4d (2p) each. More like sild, they are caught off the east coast of North America, and packed in tomato juice or vegetable oil.

Monday 11 — **"Ministry to Find 'Knockers-Up'"** An unofficial strike was called off after the Ministry of Labour promised to supply eight men from the Labour Exchange, to act as knockers-up for those workers on early shifts at the LMS Railway at Nottingham.

Tuesday 12 — **"Tea to Cost 4d a lb More"** The price of tea is to rise but the Minister hopes to maintain the domestic tea ration at 2 ounces (50gms). No more baskets except those made for tradesmen will be made and fewer wool garments are to be produced.

Wednesday 13 — **"Scarcity of Flats in London"** People who need to live in London for their war work, are finding it hard to find a home. The shortage, caused mainly by the Government's requisition of property for offices and refugees, and a subsequent rise in rental prices, is harming the war effort.

Thursday 14 — **"National Service Acts Extended"** Women who are between the age of 19, lowered from 20, and 31 will be called up for industry.

HERE IN BRITAIN

"Two Miles a Year"

The last stretch of Western Avenue, was opened and it now runs from Shepherd's Bush to Denham in Bucks. Western Avenue had the reputation of being the "most delayed road scheme in Great Britain." The first section was begun in 1920 and by the end of 1929 five miles had been completed. There was then a long delay because of the call for national economy. Eventually by 1937, 11+ miles were open and in February 1939, the last stage was begun after promised expenditure of £200,000 for the erection of a viaduct, two bridges and an embankment.

AROUND THE WORLD

"Motorists Pleasure Haunts Watched"

Driving motor cars for pleasure has been prohibited in 17 Eastern US States and has resulted in vigorous action by local officials. In Miami, motorists had to explain their presence at sports events and at Rochester, New York, petrol ration books were taken away from people who used their cars to go to a philharmonic concert. There is a scarcity of fuel oil and many buildings need oil for heating. New York is considering closing schools for a week in February instead of at Easter and hundreds of candy stores now shut at nightfall and remain closed all day on Sundays.

TOP ARMY SCROUNGERS

Before the war 218,000 tons of bones and 27,000 tons of fat were imported into Britain each year. This has now ceased and all bones and fats, which are wanted more than ever, must be collected in this country and the Army is a major source. A hundred tons of bones can be made to produce 12½ tons of grease, from which five tons of nitro-glycerine can be made, sufficient for the explosive charge of 40,000 18-pounder shells. That same 100 tons of bones can be turned into 12 tons of glue and 50 tons of fertiliser or pig food. The average amount of 'swill' per man in the British Army is 4lb a day and all fats and bones are collected.

The heavier side of the salvage work is just as efficient. Officers in charge carry a magnet in their pockets to identify any metals they find, and they love all old papers, books, letters, rags, cardboard boxes, bits of rubber, anything washed up by the sea, broken-down lorries, cars, bicycles, old prams, toys or clothes. One officer collected 100,000 used petrol tins, borrowed a steam roller to flatten the mountain and sold them on.

Unfortunately, the average soldier needs convincing of the value of this 'rubbish', so a mobile exhibition has been made showing the various forms of salvage and its value. On just one table in this exhibition is a 32-page copy of The Times from July 1937 and alongside it, a table covered with things that can be made from its pulp, including bowls and the inside part of a crash helmet. Many a dispatch rider dashes round Britain, Libya, Syria, or elsewhere, with 'the leaders, the letters, the court page, the law report, city prices and the births, deaths, and marriages' round his head.

JANUARY 15TH - 21ST 1943

IN THE NEWS

Friday 15   **"Sunday Theatre Opening"** A sharp division of opinion among actors and members of the theatrical profession was displayed at a crowded, sometimes angry, meeting in the Saville Theatre.

Saturday 16   **"Soldiers Pay to be Simplified"** The system of soldiers' pay in the British Army is now so complicated that few men have any idea what they should receive. The present rates and groups of pay, numbering around 250, will be reduced to about 50.

Sunday 17   **"Mr Lloyd George is Eighty"** The King sent a telegram of congratulations to the former Welsh Prime Minister who is now Father of the House of Commons.

Monday 18   **"Army to Eat More Potatoes"** It is the *'idle nibbling of bread'* that the Minister of Food wants to stop and see more potatoes eaten instead. The Army is to substitute 3oz of potatoes for 1oz of bread and 4oz for 1oz of flour.

Tuesday 19   **"New Rail-Bar"** The Euston station 'rail-bar' is to serve customers at the rate of 60 a minute with a variety of snacks and drinks. It is the first of a 'chain' and passengers should have time, at scheduled stops, to buy a snack and return to their compartment.

Wednesday 20   **"Reading in Comfort"** Improved lighting on trains and buses is to allow travellers to read in reasonable comfort. Lights will also be left on in railway carriages while trains are standing at stations to help passengers entering or leaving.

Thursday 21   **"Tax Returns Made Easier"** Income-tax forms for salaried workers, businessmen and farmers will be made easier to understand for the 11,000,000 people who now pay it. The forms will be in line with the simpler forms for wage earners introduced last year.

HERE IN BRITAIN

"School for Railway Clerks"

Watton House, near Hertford, the home of the late Sir Nigel Gresley, was opened as a residential training school for new station clerks on the LNER. Twenty at a time will attend for four-weeks and be given an intensive course in railway accountancy and the office routine of passenger and goods stations. There is a room equipped with a realistic booking-office, complete with tickets, telegraph instruments, ledgers and parcels scales.

This is the third wartime school but unlike the other two, who use buffet cars at stations as classrooms and boarding houses as living quarters, everything at Watton House is under one hospitable roof.

AROUND THE WORLD

"Nazis Shoot Girl Pimpernel"

The Nazis have seized and shot Leida Varunov, a heroic Russian girl aviator, who in a series of daring flights enabled 645 of her countrymen to escape from occupied parts of Leningrad and Pskov provinces.

The news was learned in the US in a letter written to her uncle shortly before her capture which revealed a premonition of her death. *"If you don't hear from me again, make an empty grave on your farm and place on it the name of your shot niece, Leida."*

In one of her flights into Nazi occupied territory, Leida rescued her own mother.

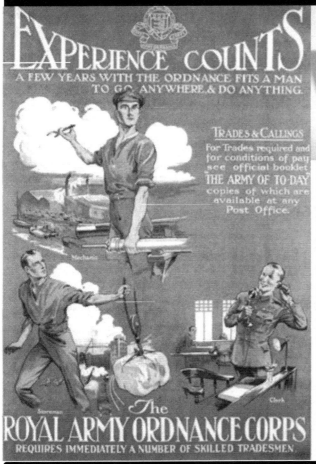

Reassembling a tank after transshipment.

A total of 179,101 packing cases, weighing, with their contents, 12,500 tons, are required to carry the equipment of a modern infantry division - apart from its food, medical stores and medical equipment. To move those packing cases 1,216 10-ton railway trucks or 4,165 three-ton lorries, are necessary. If the division is to be sent by sea, seven 10,000-ton ships will be needed and then there are still the personnel, their food, medical equipment and medical stores to be moved.

These figures are hard to believe, even by today's officers, so the Royal Army Ordinance has set up an exhibition. Everything that an infantry division carry can be seen under one roof and includes every type of infantry wireless, every type of small arm used, anti-aircraft and anti-tank artillery, all types of ammunition and all the engineering stores plus special air borne and commando equipment and various ration packs. Statistical records, diagrams and photographs giving tonnage, rail and road trucks required for transport and number of ships are on display. The RAOC not only has to store and then supply, on demand, all these things, they also supply all spare parts when required. Some of the equipment to be seen is made of several hundred parts, which, because of the dispersal of factories all over the country, come from hundreds of places and must be sorted and stored.

The RAOC does great work in saving space in ships, on rail, or road trucks. Everything handled can now be broken down and packed in cases. Great lorries go into a case; guns break down; carriers break down; motorcycles and motorcars break down. There is now nothing that cannot be broken down and packed into cases saving as much as 60% of shipping, road or rail space and the RAOC feel they have failed if the saving is any less than 25%.

JANUARY 22ND - 28TH 1943

IN THE NEWS

Friday 22   **"BBC Spills the Beans"** The BBC reported in Italy that millions of gallons of useless fuel were imported into Libya for the Italian Air force so that an Italian General could line his pockets with huge profits.

Saturday 23   **"Droitwich Spa"** The Post War Planning Committee proposes that Droitwich council should acquire the brine baths park and sea-bathing lido and develop the town as a spa.

Sunday 24   **"Babies Given Away Like Railway Parcels"** The Council for the Unmarried Mother and her Child are concerned about the number of adoptions of unwanted babies being arranged without proper safeguards.

Monday 25   **"MP Criticises Wives Who Write Too Often"** Wives and sweethearts who write three or four letters a week to their men overseas, are writing too much. Heavy mail causes delay and imposes a heavy burden on the censors.

Tuesday 26   **"Potatoes to Save Shipping Space"** The Minister of Food emphasised again the need for the nation to eat more potatoes in place of bread and called upon the Women's Institute to help tackle the problem.

Wednesday 27   **"Daily War Bill"** Parliament has voted £900,000,000 to meet expenditure to the end of the financial year and a further £1,000,000,000 for next. The daily average cost of the war has risen in recent weeks, from about £12,750,000 to about £14,000,000.

Thursday 28   **"Conchies Get More Food Than Farm Workers"** Sugar beet workers for the Essex War Agricultural committee, who are also conscientious objectors, receive £3 a week and a double meat ration in their canteen. The professional farm worker must do his work on ordinary rations.

HERE IN BRITAIN
"Women Sort the Letters"

Specially trained women of the ATS are taking over an increasing share of the work of the Army Post Office which deals exclusively with all forms of mail for the Army and the RAF overseas. There are about 2,500,000 letters a week, including about 100,000 6d (3p) air letters. The sorters' duties require a high degree of intelligence and skill as owing to the large number of different arms of the service in the British Army, and the sub-division into regiments, battalions, batteries and so on, the sorting is by no means simple. The auxiliaries each deal with about 8,000 letters a day.

AROUND THE WORLD
"News from S. Africa, USA and Switzerland"

After an excellent season with good rains, Johannesburg is sharing with other members of the Union, a glut of good, cheap fruit and vegetables.

All US civilians will have only three pairs of shoes or boots a year under a new rationing order which applies to all types of shoes and boots made in whole or in part from leather or having rubber soles.

Geneva is almost encircled by France. German occupies the north and Italy occupies the south and people here have been forbidden to use telescopes.

SPANNERS AND GUNS

Members of the light aid detachments of the Royal Electrical and Mechanical Engineers, the LADS of the REME, go into action with a tommy gun in one hand and a spanner in the other. There were no mechanically propelled vehicles in the Boer War and for the first 18 months of the Four Years' War, the only motor vehicles in use were cars, ambulances and lorries that carried supplies to some place a long way behind the front line. Then came the tanks in 1916, and mechanically propelled vehicles became a new front line of their own. At first when they broke down, they remained where they were, useless. Today all repairs to vehicles, tanks, guns, carriers, everything from the smallest watch to the latest and heaviest tank, are done by the new, young, corps, the REME. Their workshops are divided into four echelons, one working at the front line, another just behind the line, a third some way behind the line and the fourth probably at the base. The first two echelons are mobile, the third semi-static and the fourth static. The light aid detachments in the battle of Egypt, which drove Rommel from Egypt, repaired and got back into action no fewer than 1,200 tanks in the first month of that battle.

The LADS fight as well as salve and repair. Each division of the Army has nine to 12 LADS, trained to clear mine fields, fight infantry actions, demolish military objectives, recover tanks, trucks, and carriers – all under fire - from rivers, shell holes, or wherever they may have wandered. They also demolish buildings, build bridges to cross rivers or deep ravines, and get their machinery across and their wounded back. LADs are attached to tank artillery, reconnaissance regiments and to infantry brigades and every member is a skilled craftsman, artificer, fitter, welder or electrician.

JAN 29TH - FEB 4TH 1943

IN THE NEWS

Friday 29   **"The King and Queen With the RAF"** The royal couple saw Typhoons, the latest type of fighter aircraft in use by the RAF, starting off on offensive patrol when they visited stations of Fighter Command in East Anglia.

Saturday 30   **"New Life Saving Jacket for Seamen"** A bright orange life-saving jacket, conspicuous in water which has a rope loop at the back of the neck, has been approved.

Sunday 31   **"Black Market Threat to Toys"** Since the Board of Trade order prohibiting manufacture of toys retailed at more than 26s 6d (£1.30) after March 1, parents are being told of the likelihood of black marketeers cornering the expensive toy market before next Christmas.

Monday Feb 1   **"Town Having Too Many Babies"** Corby, Northamptonshire, has a birth rate five times the death rate. In the last six months, 126 children were born and only twenty-four deaths were recorded.

Tuesday 2   **"Scarcity of Wireless Sets"** Utility sets, consisting of a standard simple model, have been discussed but no decision has been reached. Meanwhile there is a growing shortage of wirelesses for the general public.

Wednesday 3   **"Chorus Girls Oppose Sunday Theatre"** Representatives said that the profession did a lot of work on Sundays and raised an enormous amount of money for charities. If there were commercial opening, they could not do that.

Thursday 4   **"Extension of Nursery Schools"** The Nursery School Association has called for local education authorities to be obliged to provide nursery school education for all children from the age of two.

HERE IN BRITAIN

"Submarines to Revert to Names"

The practice of giving each new British submarine a letter and number instead of a name, has been resented by many disappointed people and the practice is now to be discontinued. The change to a letter and number, just after the war started, is understood to have been introduced because the authorities had run dry of names beginning with 'U' for the later ships of the class which began with the Ursula, Undine and Unity. That has now been overcome by finding more 'U's such as Ullswater, Unruffled and Unseen and by also using some of the 'V's, hitherto monopolised by destroyers.

AROUND THE WORLD

"Failure of Maize Crop"

East Africa is facing a scarcity of food and particularly of maize. Irish blight, due to seed imported nearly three years ago, has wiped out the potato crop in large areas. The bean crop has failed and there is a general shortage of rice from Tanganyika. European maize growers, dissatisfied with the price of 9s a bag, have not extended their acreage whilst the flourishing pig industry has been consuming increasing quantities and consumption in general has also been steadily increasing. Finally, and devastatingly, the failure of the rains in November, locusts and the exigencies of war have exacerbated a huge reduction in supply.

CLOTHING THE ARMY

The Royal Army Ordnance Corps is responsible for all stores from guns to trousers, and their largest Ordnance clothing depot covers more than 32 acres, employing several thousand people, prominently girls. All the clothing for the British armies passes through this central depot, and stores constantly coming in, are counted and checked after being unpacked and then tested. Girls pull at seams, try buttonholes, test elastics. Cloth is tested under 100 hours of artificial sunlight and tested for the strain it will take, and socks are tested for sweat on the march. Then they are all baled and pressed again to save valuable shipping space. Great piles of hundreds of greatcoats finally make small bales and the gigantic mounds of stores creep slowly across the floors of four sheds before being made up into consignments for various armies at home and abroad.

It is impossible to enumerate the 14,000 items stored at this depot. There are 27 different sizes of boots, 14 different sizes of battle dress. There are shirts, socks, hats, knives, toothbrushes, button brushes, boot brushes, clothes brushes, braces, pants, thick and thin, housewives. Everything from 'hats, Gurkha' to 'boots, Arctic' and no article of clothing or the means to mend it has ever been asked for in vain. Millions of pairs of boots have gone to Russia and native troops in Africa have been equipped with size 13 boots, all with soles about six inches across. The fact that they have never applied for 'grindery', the name for mending materials, suggests that they still wear them round their necks! Rush jobs are never a problem. In four days, the staff pressed, baled and dispatched 1,000 miles of overcoat cloth to Russia and in a week, 20,000,000 buttons are issued to garment manufacturers and to troops direct.

FEBRUARY 5TH - 11TH 1943

IN THE NEWS

Friday 5 **"Rare Fruits for Bomb Victim Children"** Lord Mountbatten brought a rare bunch of bananas from Casablanca for Princesses Elizabeth and Margaret, but the girls asked the Queen to give them to children injured after their school in Lewisham was bombed.

Saturday 6 **"Women's Suffrage Silver Jubilee"** Women who took part in the suffrage campaign were among 300 women at a luncheon in London, to celebrate their silver jubilee.

Sunday 7 **"Tinned Fruit Back on Sale"** A new rationing period of four weeks begins, transport is a limiting factor, but in most areas the tinned fruit will include imported apricots, peaches, pears, pineapple and some grapefruit.

Monday 8 **"Mr Churchill Returns"** Since mid January, the PM has flown nearly 10,000 miles, conferring with President Roosevelt at Casablanca and visiting Turkey, Egypt and Cyprus.

Tuesday 9 **"Anti-Dim Wipers for Gasmasks"** Special impregnated cloths to prevent condensation on the eye panels of civilian gas masks are to be issued to the public. There will be no charge for the cloths which will be packed in small tin boxes.

Wednesday 10 **"Hundreds of Millions for Leisure"** Mr Bevin's Catering Wages Bill will, he says, maintain the *'communal feeding service'* which will be in great demand after the war when *"the first thing people will want, is a holiday."*

Thursday 11 **"12,000 More Nurses Needed"** Mr Bevin has begun a great recruitment drive, however, *"there must be no attempt to force a girl to be a nurse, they must be volunteers. But an attempt may be made to bring back into nursing many women who have left the profession for other work"*

HERE IN BRITAIN
"A New National Health Service"

A new and comprehensive national health service, free-of-charge to everyone who wishes to take advantage of it, with doctors on full-time salaries, who will be less interested in illness and more concerned with the maintenance of health, is recommended by the Society of Medical Officers of Health. Private enterprise (the report states) cannot provide and maintain complete hospital, medical, health and allied services, and such services conducted on a whole-time salaried basis have the dual advantages of administrative efficiency and the elimination of undesirable competition for patients.

AROUND THE WORLD
"What's In a Name?"

A baby boy born in Brooklyn, New York, has been named Adolf Hitler Mittel. The infant is normal in every other respect. The child's father is of German Austrian descent and incidentally sports an unmistakable Hitlerian moustache. *"I cannot see anything wrong in naming my son after Adolf Hitler"* he said, *"After all, lots of children are named after persons in the same category such as Napoleon and Julius Caesar."* 'G men' are expected to visit the Mittel's home to inquire why an unemployed woodcutter sees fit to rank the world's most hated ex-house painter among the world's greatest men.

BRING HOME THE BACON

The rationalisation of retail food deliveries, excluding milk and bread, has enabled 34,003 vehicles to be laid up, saving 25,000,000 gallons of petrol a year, or 36% of the petrol normally consumed in delivering groceries. The Minister of Food stated, the women of Britain by *'bringing home the bacon'* and other goods, *'though their arms might have ached at times'*, had enabled tankers to be diverted to direct war-winning work.

Soap rationing is a year old, and the Minister said of it, "*Personally, I have not noticed any serious decline in the cleanliness of the nation, but we have cut by 20% domestic consumption of soap, which was 80% of total consumption. It was the fats of which soap is made on which we wanted to economise; I have always maintained that the nation that loses its fats loses the war.*" "*Our ration*", he added, "*is three times as large as the German's and we have a choice of high-grade toilet soap, hard soap, flakes, or powder, against their hard soap or an inferior powder.*"

Although manufacturers will have sufficient materials to produce 300,000 prams this year, there is still likely to be a shortage. During the September quarter of last year (the latest figures) 168,638 babies were born in England and Wales alone and at that rate, the whole year's quota of prams will be more than filled in the first six months.

Also new, some tinned poultry has arrived from the United States and will be allocated to general hospitals, sanatoria, and maternity homes; dried fruits will be better distributed so that all shops will have an equal opportunity and a more nourishing and tastier sausage is shortly to replace the present one with an increased meat content and the addition of a new protein content from soya bean flour.

FEBRUARY 12TH - 18TH 1943

IN THE NEWS

Friday 12 **"Gandhi Fasts Again"** Mahatma Gandhi began a 21 day fast at Poona where he has been detained since his arrest following disturbances and a campaign of civil disobedience.

Saturday 13 **"£10,000,000 for New Trust"** Lord Nuffield, the founder of Morris Motors, is to start 'The Nuffield Foundation' to fund medical research and teaching, organisation and development of health services and the care and comfort of aged persons.

Sunday 14 **"Young Wives Must Have Children"** A population 'expert' from Oxford has warned that unless young mothers agree to have no less than four children now, Britain will dwindle to a *'small and unimportant State'* within 50 years.

Monday 15 **"Dinner Kept Fish off Market"** A cargo of fish landed at an east coast port but missed the last train out to its destination, because a majority of fish porters voted to take their customary hour and a half 'dinner break'.

Tuesday 16 **"Go Easy with Your Clothes"** Clothing coupons are likely to have to last beyond their termination date of July 31. No cut in the ration is contemplated but it is dependent entirely on supply which cannot be estimated at present.

Wednesday 17 **"Milk Bottle Rules"** A Ministry of Food order makes it an offence for anyone to *'misuse or wilfully destroy a milk bottle or to retain it unreasonably'*. About 2,750,000 gallons of milk are delivered daily throughout the country.

Thursday 18 **"An African Lion for Mr Churchill"** The Prime Minister has accepted the gift on condition that the lion is not kept at Downing Street or Chequers! It was previously kept by a man in his garden at Pinner but given to Regent's Park Zoo after complaints by neighbours.

HERE IN BRITAIN

"No Orchids for Miss Blandish"

The GPO no longer allows you to send flowers through the post. The first blow to the flower sending Romeos came when the Government banned acceptance of all flowers and plants by rail and then, last year, it became forbidden to send flowers or plants by parcel post.

But there was still the letter post left, and the GPO agreed to allow them to be sent in this way. But the concession has been so abused that now the ban is to be made absolute. And so, if 'Miss Blandish' still insists on orchids you will have to take them along yourself.

AROUND THE WORLD

"Power Ahead of Time"

The vast hydro-electric power plant, under construction on the Saguenay River in Quebec will equal in capacity, the mighty Boulder Dam plant in the United States, and ultimately produce at least 1,500,000 horsepower of electricity.

Two of the projected 12 generating units are already in operation. Ten thousand men have been working winter and summer on this vast project, which will be completed a year in advance of schedule. The plant will provide power for the manufacture of aluminium.

FOOD FOR OUR TROOPS

Army rations are sufficient, if there is no waste, to supply troops with four good meals a day -breakfast, mid-day, tea and supper - but meals are not good unless they are well cooked and served hot. Army chefs and instructors all attend the Army Catering Corps Training Centre at Aldershot where the equipment is equal to that of the best hotels. Before the outbreak of war, expert caterers were placed in key positions as advisers to the Army, and when war began, their number was increased by the granting of emergency reserve commissions to caterers with the requisite qualifications. About 40,000 men have already taken the Aldershot courses and by the end of the war, the three services together will probably have trained as many as 100,000 cooks.

However, field service conditions bear no resemblance to those of an ideal training centre. Army cooks must know a good deal besides cooking with the latest appliances, and Aldershot is not training cooks for the catering industry - although many thousands will be competent to take good places in the industry after the war - but for the army in barracks, in camps and on the field of war where the cook will often have to improvise. Training is done in the open-air as well as in the kitchen and here the students learn to use portable camp equipment such as Bluff and Triplex ranges and Soyer stoves, improvised oil-drum ovens and the primitive kettle trench. The Army also uses hay and insulator boxes in which food brought to cooking heat over a fire will finish cooking in a moving lorry while the unit is on the march. The Army Catering Corps is a combatant corps and in appreciation of the services of its cooks, the Army awards them extra pay.

FEBRUARY 19TH - 25TH 1943

IN THE NEWS

Friday 19   **"Helpers Wanted for Harvest"** Food production has been increased such that this year, 500,000 seasonal volunteers will be needed at harvest time. 300,000 will be rural school children but the rest, adults and children, must come from our towns as well.

Saturday 20   **"Eclipse of the Moon"** A partial eclipse of the Moon, with just over three-quarters of the diameter obscured, was visible in the early hours to a good deal of the British Isles.

Sunday 21   **"Control of Women Workers"** All women between 18 and 40, raised from 30, will now be required to obtain their employment through a local office of the Ministry of Labour and National Service.

Monday 22   **"The King's Sword for Russia"** King George has ordered a sword of honour to be offered for presentation to the Warrior City of Stalingrad, to show the admiration felt by himself and the peoples of the British Empire.

Tuesday 23   **"Fish Today"** Billingsgate had its biggest delivery since early December, including 214 tons of white fish, 90 tons of other kinds and 24 tons of shellfish. This was made possible by large Icelandic catches and more available shipping.

Wednesday 24   **"Teachers Asked to Stay in their Posts"** The Board of Education has said in a message to teachers that *'they will render their best service to the country by remaining at their posts. The care and training of the nation's children is vital not only to the country's present needs but to its future.'*

Thursday 25   **"Health Centre at Morris Motors"** War production should benefit from the opening at Morris Motors Ltd. of a new welfare building complete with medical centre and a canteen food research department.

HERE IN BRITAIN

"Gale Damage Released"

Details have been published of the worst gale in years which swept over south-eastern England during late January, with gusts reaching over 70 mph. Combined with heavy rain, the gale caused great damage over a wide area, particularly in mid-Kent, where the river Medway flooded and became a mile wide in some places. Thousands of acres of land in Kent and Sussex were flooded, young crops damaged, tree uprooted and seafronts severely battered. Many low-lying cottages and outbuildings were awash halfway up the stairs.

AROUND THE WORLD

"The Peoples' Gratitude"

Mihail Kalinin, the President of the USSR, replied to King George. *"I beg your Majesty to accept my personal gratitude for your message of high appreciation of the achievement of the Red Army ... I have informed the authorities of the City of Stalingrad of your decision to present to that city, a sword of honour, which will, without doubt, be accepted by those who took part in the defence of Stalingrad, just as by all the peoples of the Soviet Union, with gratitude as a symbol of the brotherhood in arms of the peoples of Great Britain and the Soviet Union".*

WHAT WOMEN WANT

The views of working housewives on the planning of post-war houses, have been sought by the Ministry of Health Committee on the Design of Dwellings, and what they want most is privacy. They want enough room in their own homes to give privacy from the neighbours and privacy from family members too. In country villages and in the towns, women are almost unanimous in wanting electricity and in rural areas where there is neither electricity nor gas, women want to by-pass the gas stage and go straight to electricity. In contrast, they do *not* want black lead, brass taps and dark, dust-collecting corners.

A minimum of two sitting-rooms and three bedrooms is generally accepted for a family house and there is insistence on a hot water system, a minimum size of living room of 12ft by 15ft, adequate cupboard and storage accommodation, sound-proof walls and the suction method of refuse disposal. Working women's houses should have special wash houses where clothes could be dried and mangles, plus father's garden tools now cluttering up the living space, could be stored.

These conclusions are based on the replies of more than 3,000 women, from all over England, to a list of questions prepared by the standing joint committee of Working Women's Organisations. '*The housewife,*' it states, '*looks at her house from three angles, the health of the family, the social centre for the family and her own work and leisure. She cannot be a good wife and mother unless she is also a good citizen, and for citizenship, she needs leisure from unnecessary drudgery.*' The demand for labour-saving homes was universal. The planning of the house, the working equipment and its arrangement, materials, finishes and fittings should all be designed to save unnecessary toil.

IN THE NEWS

Friday 26   **"Fewer Ladders in Rayon Stockings"** New specifications will improve the wearing quality of stockings and more cotton yarn will strengthen the heels and toes. Only 20% will be fully fashioned as men are not available to operate the heavy machinery necessary.

Saturday 27   **"Newspapers for Services"** Instead of being thrown out, newspapers are 'passed on' to men and women in the Services who, cannot obtain any of the limited supplies.

Sunday 28   **"West Country Estates for the Nation"** The Killerton and Holnicote estates are being given to the National Trust by Sir Richard Acland, MP. The estate comprises 4,500 acres of farmland and 1,500 acres of forest, just north-east of Exeter.

Mon March 1   **"Take a Week's Holiday"** The Government are advising industry that for the maintenance of health and efficiency, the usual summer holidays should be taken this year, providing they do not last longer than a week, and that also the Saturdays before each of the bank holidays at Easter, Whitsuntide, and August should also be approved holidays.

Tuesday 2   **"Wings for Victory Objectives"** London will lead the whole country in the savings campaign next week with a target of £150,000,000. Preliminary events heralding this gigantic effort begin today.

Wednesday 3   **"Commons Unable to Function"** The death of Captain Fitzroy, the Speaker of the House of Commons, brought proceedings to a temporary standstill. Without a Speaker, the House must stand adjourned until a new Speaker is appointed.

Thursday 4   **"Hospital Beds Emptied"** Hundreds of hospital beds in infectious diseases hospitals are empty because of the shortage of nurses and unless more help is obtained, mothers on war work may have to stay at home to nurse their children.

HERE IN BRITAIN
"Babies Are Like Ashtrays"

In a Commons debate this week, Major Neven-Spence pleaded for more babies saying, *"Babies are like ashtrays, you can't have too many about the house."* He suggested that there should be some arrangement whereby a soldier could get a coupon to enable him to buy a pram at a reasonable price and that we all ought to see a soldier's wife and children have something like equality with the people amongst whom they live. *'The soldier feels strongly about this matter'*, he said, *'and we should raise the allowances of service wives and children particularly.'*

AROUND THE WORLD
"Waistcoat Pocket Sized Meals"

Omelettes and aspirin size sausages were shown in Washington this week in an exhibition of new methods of sending Lease-Lend food to Britain and other countries. They were made from compressed food which will shortly replace the dehydrated food now being shipped. *"This makes a splendid meal for a full-grown man,"* said Lease-Lend Administrator Stettinius, producing a four-egg omelette pressed into a cube smaller than a match box. Then he displayed a tiny jar of granulated beef which, he said, was really several sausages and equalled 8 lbs of fresh meat.

GANDHI ENDS HIS FAST

Gandhi Starts 21-Day Fast on Citrus Juice

Viceroy Condemns New Hunger Strike

By the Associated Press

BOMBAY, Feb. 10—With India apprehensively alert, Mohandas K. Gandhi started a twenty-one-day hunger strike today—to subsist on citrus fruit juice mixed with water but not to "fast unto death" as he threatened on previous abstentions—in protest against his confinement behind barbed wire i[...] the palace of the Aga Khan at Poona.

The seventy-three-year-old, wispy patriarch imposed the limited diet upon himself after long correspondence with Lord Linlith[...] which

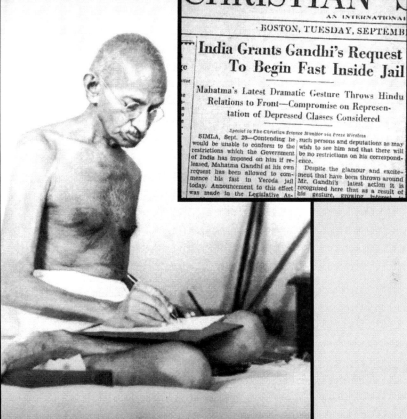

CHRISTIAN S

AN INTERNATIONA[L]

BOSTON, TUESDAY, SEPTEMB[ER]

India Grants Gandhi's Request To Begin Fast Inside Jail

Mahatma's Latest Dramatic Gesture Throws Hindu Relations to Front—Compromise on Representation of Depressed Classes Considered

Special to The Christian Science Monitor via Press Wireless

SIMLA, Sept. 20—Contending he would be unable to conform to the restrictions which the Government of India has imposed on him if released, Mahatma Gandhi at his own request has been allowed to commence his fast in Yeroda jail today. Announcement to this effect was made in the Legislative As[sembly]. such persons and deputations as may wish to see him and that there will be no restrictions on his correspondence.

Despite the glamour and excitement that have been thrown around Mr. Gandhi's latest action it is recognized here that as a result of his gesture, growing interest [...]

On 3 March, Mahatma Gandhi broke his fast by sipping a glass of diluted orange juice in the presence of doctors, officials and a few friends. He was reported to be 'weak but cheerful'. The Indian lawyer, anti-colonial nationalist and leader of a nonviolent resistance movement campaigning for India's independence from British rule, had once again employed the weapon of 'fasting'. A year after launching his 'Quit India Movement' which had led to civil disturbances, Gandhi and other Congress leaders had been arrested and imprisoned for six months in the Aga Khan's Palace in Poona. The government were now insisting that they admit and take responsibility for the troubles.

The twenty-one day-fast was never intended to be a fast unto death, Gandhi's intention was to survive the ordeal and force the government to grant him an unconditional release. He had sweet lime juice added to his drinking water which his doctor claimed was added simply to make the water palatable and surmount the nausea and excessive acidity to which Mr Gandhi was susceptible. The doctor did agree however, that the juice was necessary to avert death, but not sufficient to count as food.

The Indian government expressed regret that Mr Gandhi should think it necessary to employ such a weapon to achieve political ends, he had himself, in the past, admitted that it contained an element of coercion. They had no intention of allowing the fast to deflect their policy and as they had no way of preventing the fast, they would not take responsibility for its consequences on Mr Gandhi's health. Before breaking his fast, Mr Gandhi, in a feeble voice, joined in the singing of Hindu, Moslem and Christian hymns. Afterwards his wife handed him the glass of orange juice. Prayers to celebrate the end of the fast were said in Poona, Bombay and elsewhere.

MARCH 5TH - 11TH 1943

IN THE NEWS

Friday 5   **"London Shelter Disaster"** About 178 people were killed and 60 injured when the crowd entering a London tube shelter after the alert, tripped up and fell on top of one another, blocking a stairway. There were nearly 2,000 in the shelter.

Saturday 6   **"Farthing Nest Eggs"** Many people hoard farthings and shopkeepers need them for change. The increasing frequency of odd farthings in food prices is creating a shortage.

Sunday 7   **"Wings for Victory Week"** Greater London got the week off to a heartening start. The receipts on Saturday totalled £30,111,150.

Monday 8   **"Part-Timers Needed"** More workers are needed and the Ministry of Labour believes that we must rely on part-time work. They are calling upon married women and women with household responsibilities who cannot give a full day. Part-time solves the shopping problem, reduces absenteeism, and increases production.

Tuesday 9   **"New National Loaf"** For several weeks people have been eating a new national loaf containing home-grown barley, oats and rye. There have been no complaints and apart from the bakers, the public does not seem to have noticed.

Wednesday 10   **"Posthumous VC Found Alive!"** Although the award of the first VC for gallantry in Tunisia was gazetted as a posthumous award, the officer's sister stated that she heard from the War Office a fortnight ago that he is a prisoner of war in Italy.

Thursday 11   **"Mildest Winter for 30 Years"** The milder weather has proved a great boon to the war effort and to the fuel economy campaign. In February, London had 78 hours of sunshine. The average temperature was 44.6deg (7deg C).

HERE IN BRITAIN

"Foundation Stone Relics"

The foundation stone of the West India Docks in London has been uncovered whilst demolishing some of the warehouses that were damaged during the Battle of Britain. Two flint-glass bottles, incised with the date of the ceremony, 12 July 1800, containing the record of the stone laying were found in cavities in the stone. One bottle held the following coins: Two guineas, two half-guineas, two seven-shilling pieces, one crown, two half-crowns, two shillings, two sixpences, two four-penny pieces, two three-penny pieces, two two-penny pieces, two penny pieces, two halfpence and two farthings.

AROUND THE WORLD

"140 Years of the Sydney Gazette"

Australia's first newspaper, the 'Sydney Gazette and New South Wales Advertiser' was started in 1803. As well as shipping news, town gossip and commercial news, the newspaper contained government proclamations, regulations and detailed court appearances. George Howe, the editor and publisher of the paper had been transported to Australia for life for shoplifting in 1800. With previous experience working on the London Times, he was quickly designated Government Printer, using a small wooden printing press brought out with the First Fleet, in a lean-to shed at the back of Government House.

London embarked upon the effort to raise £150,000,000 for the war in a "Wings for Victory Week", which will serve as a model for similar weeks all over the country. The date was well chosen as indications are coming from every part of the world that the war is now rapidly reaching a climax, and is calling upon soldiers, sailors, airmen and munition workers to put forth every ounce of their strength.

Money spent on private use outside the war, diverts jobs, labour and material from the war effort. Very large sums from firms and institutions will be called for but the real test of the week's campaign will be its success in influencing the flow of 'small money', inducing people who have little out of which to save, to lay the money aside in war savings.

At the weekend, Trafalgar Square was filled with people with 'the small money'. A constant queue bought Savings Certificates and stamps and large crowds gathered to see the Stirling bomber on show near St. Paul's, the Canadian tattoo in Hyde Park and other attractions. Two 100lb bombs on which the public stuck stamps in layers will be filled with explosive after the Week and dropped on enemy territory.

Boys of 382 Squadron ATC installed a captured German rubber dinghy in one of the Trafalgar Square fountain ponds and invited the crowds to sink it with pennies. Not only was it sunk three times, but a shower of coins landed up in the water and the boys could not pick the sunken treasure up fast enough. The throng, thought to be about a million during the day, extended into Whitehall, the Strand and the entrance to the Mall. People clung precariously to every vantage point in the shadow of Nelson's Column and swarms completely hid the lions on the plinth.

MARCH 12TH - 18TH 1943

IN THE NEWS

Friday 12   **"Princess Sea Ranger"** The Queen and Princess Margaret were present when Princess Elizabeth was enrolled as a Sea Ranger. So far, training has been confined to learning signalling, keeping logs, and other nautical matters.

Saturday 13   **"Cottages for Farm Hands"** The Ministry of Works has prepared designs for the 3,000 rural cottages proposed for agricultural workers. Each will have three bedrooms, and most, a parlour and a living-room.

Sunday 14   **"£153,000,000 Raised in London"** London has already exceeded the £150,000,000 target set for 'Wings for Victory' Week and there is more money still to come.

Monday 15   **"Look Out Old Photos"** Snapshots of old churches are needed in peace time to help architects working on the reconstruction of churches damaged in air raids.

Tuesday 16   **"A Hearty Welcome"** Mr Churchill was cheered in the House of Commons when he returned for the first time since February 11th. The Prime Minister has made a good recovery from pneumonia.

Wednesday 17   **"More Milk for All"** The liquid milk ration is to be increased by half a pint to 2½ pints a week. The mild winter has helped supplies, but rather than raise allowances further, stocks of preserved milk must be built up over the summer for the forces.

Thursday 18   **"Tins of Jam Available"** Imported jam, with more fruit in it than that produced at home, is available in the shops. It is in tins instead of glass jars, which makes for easier and more economical transport.

HERE IN BRITAIN

"X Ray Pioneer"

Peace as well as war produces heroes. Harold Suggars, who has died from X-ray dermatitis at the age of 65, was the last of a gallant band of four X-ray pioneers in the London Hospital's X-ray department.

The healing value of the rays was discovered in 1896 and Suggars, a former carpenter, volunteered to become assistant to Ernest Harnack, the X-ray expert. They showed him Harnack's hands, already deeply scarred with X-ray dermatitis but he was not deterred. He knew the dangers, but suffering humanity came first and within twelve months he too noticed the first signs of the agonising, dread disease on his own skin.

AROUND THE WORLD

"Madame Chiang's Trouser Crisis"

Mme Chiang Kai-Shek, wife of the Chinese Nationalist politician, caused a crisis in the Wellesley Ladies' College, Massachusetts, where the Principal and the Faculty have been trying to ban the wearing of trousers by students.

Mme. Chiang, a guest for a night at her alma mater college, strolled over its sacred lawn— wearing a pair of exquisitely cut navy blue trousers. Women professors, who had for so long been telling their students that *'trousers are unwomanly'*, went red in the face and exchanged whispers. Then the Faculty suddenly decided to reverse its stand. They now favour trousers for girl students.

The task of collecting ordinary domestic materials in the household, belongs to local authorities, and in the first year of the war they collected 774,452 tons, in the second year 1,053,016 tons and in the third year 1,438,538 tons. By the end of 1942 the number of salvage stewards enrolled on a voluntary basis to help in collecting valuable waste material was 130,500 and school children are acting as junior salvage stewards under the guidance of members of the Women's Voluntary Service.

This week the Minister of Supply, spoke of Britain's remarkable achievements in salvage, saying that since the beginning of the war our recovery of waste paper had reached almost 3,000,000 tons; salvage of waste rubber, since the rubber scrap campaign was started last March, had considerably exceeded expectations and kitchen waste was being recovered at the rate of over 2,000 tons a day. In total, about 820,000 tons of domestic scrap has been collected during the war but the salvage of paper was still disappointing.

Nine months ago, an order was issued making it an offence to throw away or mix paper with other materials, and for quite a time, litter virtually disappeared from the streets and the countryside. But lately, careless disposal of paper has become a serious problem. However, housewives were complimented on their salvage of household scrap. Enough is collected each day to provide sufficient feeding stuff for 210,000 pigs, but a great deal is still lost because many people think that little bits are not enough to matter. From one economical home a few scraps might seem a trifle, but from millions of homes it becomes a considerable contribution, and even now, 50,000 tons of meat bones taken home every year are never heard of again and the equivalent amount must be imported, occupying valuable shipping space.

MARCH 19TH - 25TH 1943

IN THE NEWS

Friday 19   **"Freedom of the City for Mr Churchill"** The honour of the freedom of the City of London is to be conferred on the Prime Minister.

Saturday 20   **"Paid Adoptions to End"** Childless wives who try to evade call-up by adopting a baby will be stopped. The Home Office is to bring back into full operation the Provisions of the Adoption of Children Act postponed at the outbreak of War.

Sunday 21   **"The King and the Home Fleet"** The King spent four days staying aboard the King George V, flagship of the fleet. He inspected ten ships and attended an ENSA concert.

Monday 22   **"Pony Beats the Daffs-by-Rail Ban"** A pony and cart was sent one 100 miles by passenger train from Wisbech to Sheffield by passenger train. 'Tommy" hauled the cart loaded with 240 boxes of flowers back to Sheffield with daffs for the weekend market. This brought the price down in Sheffield from 8s 6d a bunch to 1s 6d.

Tuesday 23   **"Sparrow Trapping to Help Harvest"** The Ministry of Agriculture wants people to trap the house sparrow to help save the damage they do to crops – and make a tasty pie. Simmer the birds, season, add a little bacon, onion or leek and bake in a pastry case.

Wednesday 24   **"Thousands Attend Mass for Cardinal"** Queues waited for three hours outside Westminster Cathedral to attend the Requiem Mass for Cardinal Hinsley, Archbishop of Westminster.

Thursday 25   **"Housewives Bill After the War"** The Chairman of the Married Women's Association announced a Bill to define the economic status of a housewife is to be introduced. *"Their present status,"* she said, *"is that of a serf."*

HERE IN BRITAIN
"Cabbages Rotting"

Cabbages, grown to supply people with food and vitamins, are being ploughed back into the ground in the Ormskirk district of Lancashire – one of the biggest cabbage-growing areas in the country.

Others are being used to feed dairy cattle and all because, the farmers say, the 'ridiculously high' maximum prices fixed by the Ministry of Food have interfered with the demand. Prices are so high that people are not buying them and hundreds of thousands of the vegetables are being left to rot in the fields. Now the spring cabbages are coming and the Ministry will take these and not the winter crop.

AROUND THE WORLD
"Hell Hath No Fury ..."

Angry because one private soldier failed to keep a date with her, Barbara Brown cancelled the night out of more than 2,000 soldiers. The men were enjoying themselves all over Detroit, when the telephone rang at police headquarters and a strident female voice said, *"This is an Army operator speaking on behalf of General Krueger, Area Commander. He orders all soldiers now on leave to return to their bases immediately."*

The message was relayed to all police stations, the 'order' read aloud in cinemas, bars and cafes, and police toured the streets in cars shouting through loudspeakers to soldiers to return to duty at once.

FREEDOM OF THE CITY

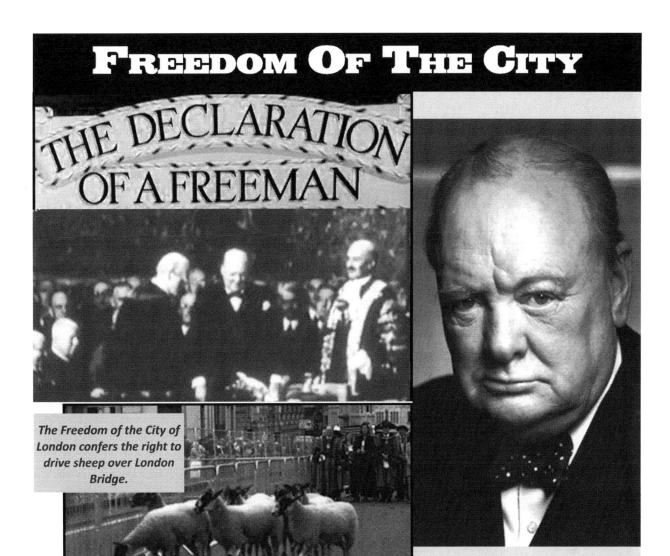

The Freedom of the City of London confers the right to drive sheep over London Bridge.

This week, it was agreed that Winston Churchill be honoured with the Freedom of the City of London. The corporation *'desired to acclaim Mr Churchill as statesman, orator, man of action and man of letters, but above all, as the inspired and accepted leader of the whole British Empire during the gravest crisis in our history.'* In 1706 his illustrious ancestor, the first Duke of Marlborough, was received by the corporation with great enthusiasm, and in return he sent a gift of 26 standards and 63 colours captured at the Battle of Ramillies to be laid up at Guildhall.

Freedom of the City was first recorded in 1237 and is closely tied to the role and status of the Livery Companies. It was, in earliest times, an essential requirement for all who wished to carry on business within the Square Mile, and as a result, the privileges attaching to the Freedom were eagerly sought, while the duties and obligations of freemen were faithfully observed.

It is still necessary to this day for all liverymen to be freemen of the City and it is the liverymen who elect the Lord Mayor and the Sheriffs of the Corporation of London. It is no longer necessary to be a freeman to work in the City, but from 1835, the freedom 'without the intervention of a Livery Company' could be purchased by nomination of two sponsors for a fee, known as a 'fine', of (now) £100, and is free to those on the electoral roll of the City. There are a number of rights traditionally but apocryphally associated with freemen including the right to drive sheep and cattle over London Bridge and carry a naked sword in public. However, these privileges are now effectively symbolic.

MARCH 26TH - APRIL 1ST 1943

IN THE NEWS

Friday 26 **"Mr Churchill at the Theatre"** The Prime Minister and Mrs Churchill went to the Strand Theatre to see 'Arsenic and Old Lace'. The audience burst into cheers and the Prime Minister responded with smiles and gave the V sign.

Saturday 27 **"Pit Schools"** To encourage boys to become miners, Pit Schools are opening in mining areas in the Rhondda Valley. At the first, at Ton Pentre, ex-miners teach boys, with lamps instead of exercise books, about safety of their future work

Sunday 28 **"Access to Coastal Areas Restricted"** A ban on 'pleasure visitors' will be in force from the coast to a depth of 10 miles inland over the whole of the East and South coasts from the Humber to Penzance.

Monday 29 **"Forces' Cheap Fares Return"** The ban on Service men and women booking cheap rail fares to places over 50 miles from the booking station is to be lifted. Imposed last September the ban reduced the number of personnel crowding long-distance winter trains when going on short leave.

Tuesday 30 **"The Vanishing Tramp"** Largely owing to war-time conditions the tramp is disappearing from the roads and casual wards of England and Wales. Many have taken employment or gone into the forces.

Wednesday 31 **"Home Grown Meals"** Two out of three meals eaten in Britain are now home-produced saving on shipping and imports. For every 100 tons of food produced before the war, we now produce about 170 tons.

Thurs April 1 **"The RAF is 25 Years Old Today"** To celebrate their twenty-fifth birthday, the King, for the first time, approved the RAF mounting a guard at Buckingham Palace for four days.

HERE IN BRITAIN

"Swinging Reveille"

Tired of being abused by his fellow soldiers every morning when he woke them with his Reveille, a US bugler in Britain played the 'get-out-of-bed' call in swing and 'lights out' in soothing lullaby time. Now US Army authorities have approved it, and hope that others may do the same. Private Zylman has always been a trumpeter. He was one of the shining stars of Tommy Tucker's American dance orchestra in New York and felt his talents were wasted when, after standing ankle-deep in mud on cold, misty mornings, he was greeted with shouts of "Will somebody strangle that guy!"

AROUND THE WORLD

"Butchers Cleaned Out"

The people of New York, in a rush to buy meat before meat rationing came into effect, virtually cleaned out the butchers' shops and wholesalers' stocks. Police had to disperse 2,000 butchers who later staged a meeting which nearly became a riot when they could get no more supplies. *"We must have meat to feed the defence workers,"* they cried, gathering menacingly round a lorry which had been filled with meat for a big firm of chain stores. They claimed the lack of meat to be an artificial rather than actual shortage because of a breakdown in the distribution system.

THE ROYAL AIR FORCE

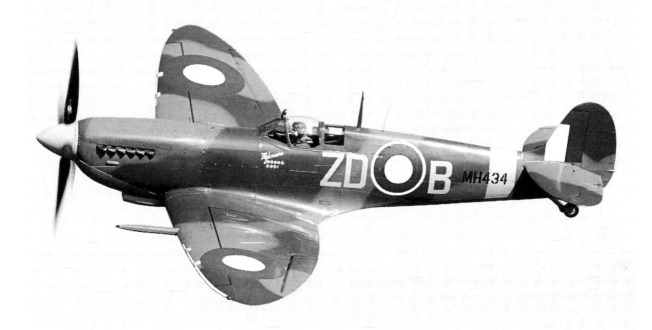

The RAF Spitfire

Mr Churchill has been awarded his honorary wings, the flying badge of the Royal Air Force. The honour was conferred this week on the twenty-fifth anniversary of the formation of the RAF, formed at a critical period of the last war, by the amalgamation of the Army's and Navy's flying wings, the Royal Flying Corps and the Royal Naval Air Service. It came into being after three years and eight months of war and its twenty-fifth birthday falls after three years and seven months of an even greater war.

When the war of 1914 started, the aeroplane was a new and untried weapon, strictly limited in its uses and not sure of its role. Rapidly it developed both as a weapon of offence and defence. When the allies mounted their counter-offensive in 1918, the RAF was able to concentrate 1,290 first-line aircraft against its opponents' 340, and, enjoying this air superiority, was able to disrupt the Germans' communications and harass their troops by low flying attacks. When the Armistice came, the RAF was the greatest air force in the world, both numerically and in quality of equipment, possessing more than 200 squadrons, 22,647 aircraft of all, 103 airships and a total strength of 291,000 officers and men. After the war the Service shrank to a shadow of its former self but managed to keep many members possessing a pioneering spirit, which in turn, maintained the high standards and increased the prestige of British aviation throughout the world.

At the beginning of this war, we had far fewer planes than Germany and the country has undergone a massive drive to build Spitfires and Hurricane fighters, and Wellington, Whitley and Hampden bombers. All technically superior to the German planes, but it was, nonetheless, a dangerous situation until the Battle of Britain had been won.

APRIL 2ND - 8TH 1943

IN THE NEWS

Friday 2   **"Turn the Heating Down"** Central heating is to be strictly rationed during the summer. With a few exceptions, no fuel may be used for heating in shops, offices, flats or non-industrial establishments.

Saturday 3   **"Put Your Clocks on Tonight"** The clock is already one hour ahead of Greenwich Mean Time and overnight the additional hour comes into force meaning double summertime will be two hours ahead of GMT.

Sunday 4   **"Summertime Causes River and Cycle Rush"** The number of boats on the upper reaches of the Thames was a record for the first Sunday in April, whilst thousands of cyclists from London poured down the main roads to Southend.

Monday 5   **"Bicycles for Lonely Troops"** The people of Norfolk have given £500 to buy bikes for soldiers on lonely searchlight and gun sites who are unable to enjoy their off-duty hours, being stuck miles from the nearest town or village.

Tuesday 6   **"New National Salvage Campaign"** 23 Counties will take part in the campaign designed to be the most intensive salvage sweep ever attempted in this country. Every scrap of wastepaper, metal, bones, rags, rubber and kitchen waste is wanted.

Wednesday 7   **"I Do Again"** Lana Turner, the film star who was divorced from her husband Stephen Crane last month, has remarried him in Mexico. Miss Turner is expecting a baby and said, *"I love Stephen very much and want our baby to have a normal life with its father."*

Thursday 8   **"Sudden Shoals of Fish"** After months of scarcity, supplies of fish made a sudden jump to almost glut levels. Housewives could not know this and made no extra demands of fishmongers. To avoid waste, the Ministry temporarily removed the controls on restaurants.

HERE IN BRITAIN

"Shorter Black-Out for Summer"

The summer reduction of the black-out period will take effect on May 2. For most of the year the black-out time extends from half an hour after sunset to half an hour before sunrise, but from then until the second Saturday in August it is reduced to one hour after sunset to one hour before sunrise in Scotland and the counties of Northumberland, Durham and Cumberland, and from three-quarters of an hour after sunset to three-quarters of an hour before sunrise in the rest of England and Wales. This year double summertime has begun a month earlier than the period of reduced black-out.

AROUND THE WORLD

"Monty the Mouse"

Canadian squadrons went on a sweep over France and one of the pilots felt a scratching inside his helmet. The Spitfire climbed past 18,000ft, and the scratching stopped. When they landed, a mouse was found dead inside the helmet. It had apparently broken into the pilot's locker and crawled inside.

Accused of animal cruelty by his mates, the pilot is tasked with designing an oxygen mask for any other mice he wants to take on sweeps with him! NB. Pilots turn their oxygen on between 12,000 – 15,000 ft otherwise they pass out. Monty lasted longer!

SUITS OF ARMOUR

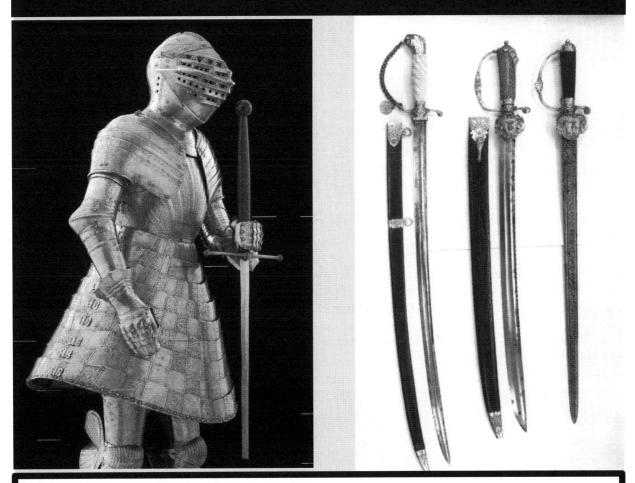

An important collection of armour and arms from Norton Hall, near Daventry has been acquired for presentation to the Armouries of the Tower of London. The collection was formed by Beriah Botfield (1807-1863), a member of Parliament for Ludlow, who inherited the family's extensive coal mining and iron making business in Shropshire, but is known chiefly as a naturalist, antiquary and bibliographer. In 1858, he had a stone cross erected near the Wales–England border on Shadwell Hill, to commemorate a pedlar named William Cantlin who was robbed and murdered there in 1691.

The Norton Hall collection is particularly rich in early firearms and contains also six complete suits of armour and four half-suits, besides numerous swords, halberds and crossbows. Of the suits of armour, the earliest is a Gothic example of about 1470, and there are also two highly decorated suits of about 1550, probably made for the Spanish Court. One of these has on the breast a plaque etched with the insignia of the Order of the Golden Fleece, and is perhaps an early work of Anton Peffenhauser, of Augsburg.

The guns and pistols include many very beautifully designed and decorated weapons, among them a series of pistols made at Brescia in the mid-seventeenth century and particularly slender and elegant, two French wheel-lock pistols made for Louis XIII. Other specially notable firearms are a late seventeenth-century German wheel-lock gun with a hunting scene, showing a noble huntsman, his keeper, two hounds, a stag and a doe set in a landscape, vividly etched on the lock plate; a fowling piece made for Charles IV of Spain and a flint-lock gun made by the Rev Alexander Forsyth, a Scottish Presbyterian minister, who, in 1809, revolutionised warfare by inventing the percussion lock.

APRIL 9ᵀᴴ - 15ᵀᴴ 1943

IN THE NEWS

Friday 9   **"Italian Prisoners Have Bikes?"** In Lincolnshire, complaints have been made that while war workers have great difficulty obtaining bicycles, Italian prisoners of war in the rural areas have been seen riding almost new machines to farm work in the district.

Saturday 10   **"Holidays at Home Again"** To induce Londoners to spend their summer holidays at home, the LCC will provide opera and musical comedy, ballet, circuses, concert parties, band performances, fairs, swimming galas, boxing tournaments and dancing.

Sunday 11   **"The Queen's Speech"** Queen Elizabeth broadcast a message to the women of the Empire. She paid tribute to the astonishing work and quiet heroism of women in helping to win the war.

Monday 12   **"WREN's Anniversary Parade"** The fourth anniversary of the revival of the Women's Royal Naval Service was celebrated in London by a ceremonial parade of 1500 Wrens at Horse Guards Parade. The Queen took the salute at a march past at Buckingham Palace.

Tuesday 13   **"Beer and Baccy Up"** The decision to raise prices was taken by the trades concerned following the increase in taxation announced in the Budget.

Wednesday 14   **"Lloyd George's Letter"** To every householder who applies for coal in excess of the ration: *"The needs of the war must have priority but there will be just enough left over to meet the essential needs of domestic consumers, provided you and others continue to burn as little as you possibly can."*

Thursday 15   **"Pre-War Scale of Musical Plays"** The Government has warned theatre managers to reduce the numbers of artists, chorus girls and boys necessary to stage pre-war standards. The applications for deferment, retention of services and clothing coupons is detrimental to the war effort.

HERE IN BRITAIN
"Coupons Rule"

The Board of Trade has announced that employers are now legally entitled to collect coupons from workers to get towels for use of the staff. Socks of foot length up to nine and a half inches will require only one coupon, irrespective of leg length or material. Babies' day gowns will now be rated at the same coupon value as night gowns. Reconditioned Service clothing is also now on the ration. An Army greatcoat is rated at eight coupons, battle-dress suit at six coupons and an Observer Corps type overall at four coupons.

AROUND THE WORLD
"Black Market Take Over"

Former associates of the gangster Al Capone have taken over huge packing plants and distribution warehouses and are now outbidding legitimate traders in all food markets. In Chicago 'Black Market Incorporated' owns seven large meat packing plants. The authorities in New York and New Jersey neighbourhoods raided seven companies who were charged with bringing 5,000 tons of this meat into New York between December 16 and January 31 and selling it at £500,000 above regulation prices.

HERITAGE PORTRAITS

Clockwise from the top left:
**Nelson
Drake
Churchill
Pitt the Younger**

During the war the exhibition at Underground stations in London of attractive pictures of beauty spots for the delight of the holiday maker has had to give place to the posting of utilitarian bills giving strictly essential information. A new series of posters now displayed depart from this note of austerity and give a direct message appropriate to wartime. The series is entitled 'Our Heritage' and consists of portraits of four men famous for their service to the country - Drake, Nelson, Pitt the Younger and Mr Churchill, with excerpts from their prayers or speeches on great occasions.

Drake's prayer on the day he sailed into Cadiz in 1587. Nelson's prayer on the eve of Trafalgar in 1805 and Pitt the Younger speaking in the House of Commons in April 1804. The quotation chosen from Mr Churchill's speeches are the words spoken after the collapse of France in June 1940.

The posters carry the statement that they have been 'Printed for the passengers and staff of London Transport to recall other occasions of the nation's will and high purpose.' They are executed in pen and ink and wash by Robert Austin, ARA, who is working as an official war artist. Issued with this series is a larger poster, setting out in old English lettering the text of the Atlantic Charter issued in August 1941, setting out the American and British goals for the world after the end of this war.

No territorial aggrandisement, no territorial changes made against the wishes of the people, restoration of self-government to those deprived of it, reduction of trade restrictions, global co-operation to secure better economic and social conditions for all, freedom from fear and want, freedom of the seas, abandonment of the use of force and disarmament of aggressor nations.

APRIL 16ᵀᴴ - 22ᴺᴰ 1943

IN THE NEWS

.Friday 16   **"Stay Put at Easter"** People are being urged not to travel at Easter unless it is 'absolutely necessary'. The trains will be crowded, uncomfortable, and you may be stranded.

Saturday 17   **"Women for Home Guard"** Women are to be recruited to the Home Guard in the ratio of 20 to 100 men. Safeguards are set out so that the civil defence services will not be affected by the loss of women recruits.

Sunday 18   **"Demand Increasing for Women's Land Army"** Even with 60,000 workers, still more volunteers are needed by farmers who can billet them. The largest demand is for milkers.

Monday 19   **"Vatican Broadcasts to Russia"** For the first time, Vatican radio broadcast directly in Russian with the Pope's Easter letter asking Christians to pray for peace during May.

Tuesday 20   **"Gas Works for Sale"** The gas works in Eye in Suffolk, where the local council has given up gas for electricity, are going for a 'modest price'. *"It is not a highly desirable residence,"* said the Town Clerk, *"but it might be used as a small cinema or dance hall."*

Wednesday 21   **"Princess Elizabeth is Seventeen"** Because her birthday fell in Holy Week, the Princess did not hold a party to celebrate her birthday but spent the day in the country with the King and Queen and Princess Margaret.

Thursday 22   **"Book Salvage"** 417,905 books were collected in the national salvage drive in Oxford. Many valuable or rare books were taken by the Bodlean library, but the majority will be pulped, and the rest go to the forces, children's hospitals and war damaged libraries.

HERE IN BRITAIN

"Roads for the Future"

A skeleton system of high-speed roads, referred to as 'motorways', to accommodate long-distance mechanical transport is advocated by the Institution of Highway Engineers. The motorways, it is suggested, should be reserved for motor traffic only and there should not be access to them except at relatively infrequent intervals. All intersecting roads should be carried over or under them; gradients should be easy; transition curves, both horizontal and vertical, should be used and, on horizontal curves, super elevation for speeds up to 100 miles an hour should be applied; they should have a good non-skid surface and land should be reserved for refreshment rooms.

AROUND THE WORLD

"130 Days Alone on a Raft"

A Chinese seaman was rescued after 130 days alone on a raft in the middle of an ocean after the ship in which he was travelling was torpedoed and sank in the middle of the night.

He managed to clamber onto a raft and next day he saw another raft not far away with five or six other survivors, but this disappeared during the next night.

Emergency rations kept him going for the first 60 days but by the time these were gone he had become expert at catching birds and fish and rigged up equipment to collect rainwater.

MAUNDY MONEY

George VI, did not attend the Maundy service between 1940 and 1944, his place being taken in most years by the Lord High Almoner, Cosmo Gordon Lang, Archbishop of Canterbury.

The distribution of Maundy Money, which takes place on the Thursday before Easter, is the modern development of an ancient ceremony said to be derived from when Christ washed his disciples' feet the evening before his crucifixion. In Britain the service goes back many centuries and Elizabeth I personally took part in 1572, in the hall at Greenwich. On that occasion a laundress, the sub-Almoner and the Lord High Almoner washed the feet of the poor people, and the feet then being, apparently, thoroughly clean, were again washed and kissed by the Queen herself. She then distributed broadcloth for the making of clothes and fish, bread and wine.

Royalty continued to take part but the last time the foot-washing ritual took place was in 1685. Several changes have taken place since then. Clothing was substituted for broadcloth for the women but that was stopped in 1724 and money was given in lieu. In 1837 William IV agreed to give the pensioners thirty shillings in lieu of all provisions.

For many years the ceremony took place in Whitehall Chapel moving later to Westminster Abbey and this year the distribution was made in Westminster Abbey by Archbishop Lord Lang, Lord High Almoner to the King and the congregation included a party of soldiers and airmen of the Dominions forces who were given privileged places. The pensioners receive some of the world's most interesting coins presented in a small leather purse, with as many pence as the monarch has years of age - 45 - and the recipients themselves number as many men and as many women as the monarch has years. In the days before base metal money, the amount was made up from silver pennies, twopences, threepences and fourpences and are still, today, struck in silver and polished like proof coins.

APRIL 23ʀᴅ - 29ᴛʜ 1943

IN THE NEWS

Friday 23 "Beside the Seaside" South coast resorts, open at Easter for the first time in three years, were not overly busy but many of the northern coast towns were crowded with 80,000 in Blackpool alone.

Saturday 24 "No Proxy Weddings" The Government has said 'no' to men serving overseas being able to marry by proxy. The MP who tabled the matter said the decision *"would label many innocent babies as illegitimate and cause hardship and sorrow to thousands of decent British girls*

Sunday 25 "Sunrise Easter Service" American soldiers, airmen, Red Cross nurses and some naval officers voluntarily paraded in Hyde Park at an Easter sunrise service. There was a congregation of about 1,000, but few civilians.

Monday 26 "A Welcome Break" Britain, on the fourth Easter at war, was symbolised this bank holiday at Stamford Bridge where an enormous holiday crowd saw non-stop football for three hours. Two matches between the Belgian Army and the Norwegian Forces and then between the British Army and the RAF.

Tuesday 27 "Coupons for Curtains Please" The Board of Trade has been urged to issue special coupons for the renewal of towels and curtains as a 'household' purchase rather than the 'housewife's' personal purchase.

Wednesday 28 "Absenteeism in Schools" The Government needs to take drastic action. Pre-war attendance is a long way from being re-established and without intervention, very soon a large proportion of the senior school population would be leaving school semi-illiterate.

Thursday 29 "Lady Nelson" The former cruise liner sunk by torpedoes in St Lucia a year ago has been resurrected by the Canadian Government and fitted out as a spotless floating hospital with accommodation for 500 patients ready to repatriate Canadians wounded in Europe.

HERE IN BRITAIN

"Time For Tea Making Lessons"

Standardised excellence in tea-making is the aim of a 16-page booklet, complete with diagrams and photographs, which has just been issued for the guidance of the staffs of Navy, Army and Air Force Institutes. It points out that if one gallon of tea were wasted each day, through over- making, in every NAAFI canteen, there would be a total wastage in a year, not counting fuel, over the whole organization of more than 50,000,000 cups of tea, and that this is equivalent to £250,000 in cash. *"The tea leaf,"* it is stated, *"only yields its best when it is subjected to water at boiling point—ie. bubbling fiercely."*

AROUND THE WORLD

"New Jazz Tune"

Stirred into delirious antics by a new jitterbug tune called 'Two O'Clock Jump' thousands of boys and girls are storming Broadway. Youths mostly 14,15 and 16 clamour for entrance into the cinema several times daily where Harry James's band is featuring the new jazz tune. Jivers as they are called, start forming a queue at 4am and on the first day they shattered windows and sent one policeman to hospital with two fractured ribs. Police are asking the cinema whether it is possible to replace 'Two O'Clock Jump' with something more soothing like 'Three O'Clock in the morning'.

Famed in song and as a spa, Ilkley can now claim new recognition as a pioneer in practical planning. It was the chairman of the local war savings committee who, shocked by the town's shabby centre, opened an attack and promoted a competition of this ancient town in Wharfedale.

Many of the schemes for improvement submitted and judged by an expert committee of assessors, have been put on exhibition in Maddox Street in London. Ilkley's problem concerns a site lying on both sides of the river Wharfe which contains the remains of the Roman fort of Olicana, the parish church, cottages known as the 'Castle', Ilkley Bridge, the New Bridge and a large area of open space - now shabby and unsightly with nondescript buildings, a caravan camp and untidy trade signs. As an announcement at the exhibition points out, *'Ilkley has no excuse for shabbiness. It is a small but prosperous community and has been outstanding in its war savings campaign, in which it has already contributed some £2,500,000 . . .'*

This competition was won by a serving soldier whose designs, together with a large model of his scheme and the designs of many other competitors, are on show. There are also many attractive large photographs of Wharfedale. The competition attracted a lot of interest and in spite of war duties preventing many applicants from finishing their designs, 78 were received. All of these will be shown later at Ilkley. Meanwhile, a selection is being shown in London as a lesson and a stimulus to other town planners and show how local amenities can be enhanced.

The exhibition was opened by the Parliamentary Secretary to the Ministry of Town and Country Planning who spoke of the *'glory of the Yorkshire dales'* and then made the 'awful confession' that he had never been to Ilkley.

APRIL 30TH - MAY 6TH 1943

IN THE NEWS

Friday 30 — **"Campaign Against Tuberculosis"** The advent of miniature radiography has meant a big step forward in the campaign against tuberculosis, particularly in the ability to detect the disease's presence at an early stage when there is a good chance of recovery.

Sat May 1 — **"48 Hurt in Rail Crash"** Fifteen women and thirty-three men, including eight stretcher cases, were taken to hospital after a rush-hour train from Tunbridge Wells collided with buffer stops at Victoria Station.

Sunday 2 — **"New Order for Part-Time Workers"** More people, mainly women up to the age of 45 with family responsibilities which do not permit them to take full-time work, will soon be directed into part-time work in industry and business.

Monday 3 — **"Bath Assembly Rooms Restoration"** The famous Assembly Rooms, partly destroyed in air raids a year ago, are to be restored. Just before the war, Bath corporation spent £50,000 on their redecoration and refurnishing.

Tuesday 4 — **"New Constable of the Tower"** Field-Marshal Sir Philip Chetwode was installed for the next five years as Constable of the Tower of London.

Wednesday 5 — **"Housekeeping Savings Belong to the Husband"** An Oxford County Court Judge deemed that money saved by a wife out of the housekeeping, for clothes, tablecloths or having the occasional hairdo, is legally the property of their husbands.

Thursday 6 — **"New Record for Atlantic Crossing"** A BOAC Captain has made a record flight from Newfoundland to Britain. He covered the 2,200 miles in 7 hours 16 minutes, 24 minutes less than the previous best time.

HERE IN BRITAIN
"Cheap Baccy For Pensioners"

The Labour Party is to use the Budget discussions to press on with its campaign for increased old age pensions. Knowing this will be turned down, they will then suggest a 'token' in the form of a coupon for old age pensioners to buy tobacco at a cheap rate.

It would be a small gesture and cost little. *'It is a tragedy when a man in the evening of his life, is unable to enjoy the solace of a pipe of tobacco. Even an ounce of tobacco a week is beyond the purchasing power of someone struggling to exist on a few shillings a week.'*

AROUND THE WORLD
"Debut of the Duke of Alba's Daughter"

The coming-out ball for the Duke of Alba's only child, Donia Maria del Rosario Cayetana, Marquesa de San Vicente del Barco, began just before midnight and lasted till dawn, at the Palace of the Duenas in Seville and was the most brilliant social event since the days of the monarchy. Over 3,000 guests representing many walks of life in Spain were present. The 15th century Mudejar palace provided a perfect setting, with its floodlit Moorish Garden, where people danced to modern music or listened to typical Andalusian folk-music. Among the distinguished guests was Mr Yencken, the Minister, who represented the British Embassy.

CONSTABLE OF THE TOWER

The Constable of the Tower of London and the ceremonial gold key.

The new Constable of the Tower of London was installed this week in a ceremony that reaches back almost 900 years. About 20 Yeoman Warders formed a circle on the grass, dressed in scarlet and gold with tricolour rosettes and ribbons. In the centre stood the Chief Warder and near him the Yeoman Gaoler carried the gleaming processional axe. The Lord Chamberlain came out from the King's House carrying a ceremonial gold key on a red velvet cushion. Behind him walked in procession the new Constable, the Lieutenant of the Tower and the Resident Governor and Major of the Tower. The band struck up a Royal Salute in honour of the King's representative, who had come *'in the King's name and on His Majesty's behalf, to deliver the Keep and Custody of His Majesty's Palace and Fortress of the Tower.'*

The role was established by William the Conqueror around 1078 and the holder was then known as the Keeper of the Tower and historically, he controlled the operation, upkeep and security of the Tower and everyone who lived and worked within it. He was also responsible for the Tower's, often famous, prisoners. In return for his service, the Constable was given the right to seize any swan that swam under London Bridge; any horse, ox, cow, pig or sheep that fell into the Thames from the bridge and any cart that fell into the Tower of London's moat. Every ship that came upstream to the city had to moor at Tower Wharf to unload a portion of its cargo for the Constable and although the role is largely ceremonial today, this tradition is still upheld at the annual Ceremony of the Constable's Dues. When a ship of the Royal Navy visits the Port of London, the Captain presents a barrel of wine, his 'Dues', to the Constable on Tower Green.

MAY 7TH - MAY 13TH 1943

IN THE NEWS

Friday 7   **"Pay-As-You-Earn"** A Group of Conservative MPs have given support to the principle of relating the income-tax of both manual and non-manual workers to present rather than the past year's earnings.

Saturday 8   **"Fitness Centre for Miners"** The formal opening of the Fitness Centre for Miners in Gleneagles indictes the importance attached by the Government to the waste of physique and the need for a scientific system of rehabilitation after injury or illness.

Sunday 9   **"More Rations for Backyarders"** Domestic poultry keepers have a larger ration of feeding stuffs for their hens. They are asked not to keep more hens, but to use the additional meal to get better egg production.

Monday 10   **"National Blood Tests"** Staff of the Ministry of Health are the first to undergo a blood test, two drops taken from the earlobe, to check the haemoglobin content as part of the continuous check kept on the state of national nutrition.

Tuesday 11   **"Prime Minister in Washington"** Mr Churchill has arrived to renew discussions with President Roosevelt. This is their fifth meeting and carries with it the presage of fate, for each has been followed by momentous events.

Wednesday 12   **"Sea Water for Drinking"** It has been found that distillation is the most successful procedure and arrangements have been made to equip all lifeboats of ocean-going merchant ships with stills.

Thursday 13   **"Record £20 million for the Red Cross"** The Red Cross and St John Fund reached a record level, including, £5,250,000 in pennies through the 'penny-a-week fund'.

HERE IN BRITAIN

"New Food Ration Books"

From July, the new ration book will simplify transactions for both shopper and shopkeeper and include the personal points coupons (detachable) for chocolates and sweets as well as ration and points coupons. There will be less cutting out of coupons for the shopkeeper, and less writing of names and addresses for both him and the shopper.

Coupons for cod liver oil and fruit juices for children are a new feature. With the tea coupons go three sets of coupons marked K, L, and M, each covering 52 weeks. What they are for is not indicated!

AROUND THE WORLD

"Our Films in Stockholm"

British war films are so popular in the Swedish capital that some of them are running at several cinemas simultaneously. The film 'Mrs. Miniver', which had a triumphant run at the city's largest cinema is now showing at four cinemas, with eight packed houses every night. Demand for tickets is enormous and the film is in its twentieth week. 'This Above All' is on at three cinemas and is in its twelfth week. Noel Coward's film, 'In Which We Serve' is running for the seventh week and has had to be transferred to the largest cinema in Stockholm, the Palladium.

FIRST STARS AND STRIPES

At a ceremony at Claridges in London, the Commander in Chief of the US Naval Forces in Europe received from the women of Yorkshire, a replica of the very first Stars and Stripes to come to Europe. The original ensign, made by the women of New Hampshire, was hoisted in the ship 'Ranger', commanded by Captain John Paul Jones on July 4, 1777 - the first anniversary of the Declaration of Independence.

Two years later, Captain Jones, flying his flag from a converted French merchantman, the 'Bon Homme Richard', and carrying it for the first time into English waters, fought a tremendous battle with the British frigate HMS Serapis which was guarding a convoy bound from Hull for the Baltic. The battle was fought close to the Yorkshire coast. The Americans managed to board the British vessel, whose captain struck his own flag when three-quarters of his crew were dead but soon afterwards, the 'Bon Homme Richard' sank, a rare case of a vessel being sunk by the guns of the ship she vanquished. Their flag was carried to the bottom under the Yorkshire cliffs.

The replica of the flag has been sewn by women from all parts of Yorkshire and this, together with a plaque, is destined for the US Naval Academy at Annapolis. After the flag had been presented, the Commander asked if there was any more fitting way in which the women of Yorkshire could have expressed the healing of past wounds, faith in the present and hope for the future. In 1779 the Stars and Stripes came to Europe as a belligerent; in 1917 it came back to fight side by side with the Union Jack and in 1943, *'the Americans have again fought with us, side by side, to make men free against those who would make men slaves.'*

MAY 14TH - 20TH 1943

IN THE NEWS

Friday 14 **"Thousands of Idle Bus Workers"** The General Workers' Union have ordered the bus men and women on strike in about a dozen towns in Yorkshire, the Midlands and the south, to return to work at once pending a national conference to discuss their pay claim.

Saturday 15 **"The Sport of Kings"** The King and Queen were present at the one-day May meeting held at Ascot. This was the first meeting to be held at Ascot since the war began and the first time that their Majesties had been there since 1938.

Sunday 16 **"Empire Youth Sunday"** At Buckingham Palace, the Queen addressed 2,000 members of the youth detachment of the British Red Cross Society and cadets of the St John Ambulance Brigade who paraded on the lawns.

Monday 17 **"Workmen Find Ancient Boat"** A 24' long boat, hollowed out of the trunk of a great oak tree and believed to belong to the period 800BC, has been dug up in the bed of an old river in Ancholme Valley, near Scunthorpe.

Tuesday 18 **"Miners Work Extra Day"** Scottish miners have decided to work an extra day to produce an additional 50,000 tons of coal, as a tribute to our armies for their African victories.

Wednesday 19 **"More Letters to Japan's Prisoners"** Letters may now be sent to prisoners of war and civilian internees in Siam, Burma, the Philippines, Java, Sumatra and Borneo. No postage stamps are needed.

Thursday 20 **"A May Winter in the Lakes"** Severe weather has brought the Lake District a miniature winter. During the first 10 days came the greatest snowfall, the heaviest rainfall, the worst floods and the most destructive frost of the year.

HERE IN BRITAIN

"Water Fit for a King"

When the King inspected an Army division in the Eastern Command, he saw Royal Engineers demonstrating how the Army makes itself independent of water supplies by purifying river water and making it fit to drink. Watching the Sappers working their sterilising plant, the King asked to sample the water.

He drank from a tankard pure, clear water which only a few minutes before had been taken, brackish and muddy, from the river. *"It is very good,"* the King said, adding with a smile, *"but you had better ring me up tomorrow to make sure that it was all right."*

AROUND THE WORLD

"Premiers Triumph"

Mr Churchill scored one of his greatest personal triumphs when he spoke to the world from the United States Congress in Washington. A roar of cheering and shouting lasted for three minutes when he appeared in the House of Representatives, and his speech was constantly interrupted by roars of applause. Many Congressmen said the speech was the greatest of his career. Early on he delighted his listeners with his assurance that *"we British are not interested only in the war against Germany. We have at least as great an interest as the US in the unflinching and relentless waging of war against Japan."*

THE HOME GUARD

In the presence of the King and Queen, the Home Guard took over the guard at Buckingham Palace on 'Home Guard Sunday', as a mark of honour on the third anniversary of their formation. They relieved the Scots Guards on duty in the morning and then the steel-helmeted sentries in the Palace forecourt, carried out the traditional ceremonial duties with the steadiness of regular soldiers. Later at a demonstration in Hyde Park, after a march past, members of several Home Guard battalions gave a demonstration of weapon firing, including the spigot mortar, and other aspects of training including Home Guard battle drill.

The Home Guard was originally formed on 14 May 1940 when the Secretary of War, Anthony Eden, broadcast a radio appeal to the nation. The appeal called for all men between the ages of 17 and 65 to enrol as Local Defence Volunteers (LDV) as a precaution against enemy parachute landings in the event of an invasion. By the end of July 1940, over one million men had signed up and the name was changed to something more inspiring - the Home Guard.

The volunteers are those unable to join the regular army. They are either too young, too old or working in reserved occupations and while the age for the volunteers was meant to be 17 to 65, this is not strongly enforced with many older soldiers joining. At first it was a disorganised militia, Eden had told those interested to register at the police station closest to them but gave no further details, and identification was solely by the wearing of an armband. Now the Home Guard has weapons, uniforms and extensive training for the responsibilities of defending key targets in the country including factories, beaches and explosive stores. The Home Guard is our last line of defence.

IN THE NEWS

Friday 21   **"Smaller Knives and Forks"** Standard cutlery is to be manufactured in 'rationed' sizes. There will be maximum material-saving lengths for carving knives, forks, bread knives and steels and one size of table knives, tablespoons, dessertspoons and teaspoons.

Saturday 22   **"Big Identity Card Round Up"** Civil and military police stopped cars, cyclists and pedestrians and visited dance halls, pubs, clubs and cafes. Hundreds of names and addresses were taken, and many people escorted to police stations.

Sunday 23   **"Worse Than Piggeries"** *"I should be happy to think that all our schools were as adequate as the best of our racing stables and the most modern piggeries, but they are not"*, said the Director of Education for West Sussex.

Monday 24   **"Ration Books Muddle"** The distribution of 47,000,000 new identity cards and ration books began amid an outcry from people living in rural areas obliged to collect their new documents from centres miles from their homes.

Tuesday 25   **"A Cloak of Comfort"** Today is the third anniversary of the start of the foreign relations department of the Red Cross and St John War Organisation. It was set up to make inquiries for missing civilians of all nationalities in enemy or enemy occupied territory.

Wednesday 26   **"New Cap Badge"** The new cap badge of the Parachute Regiment will be worn by all parachute troops instead of the badge of the Army Air Corps, of which it forms a part. The design is a parachute on spread wings, with the royal crest above.

Thursday 27   **"More Savings"** 'Wings for Victory' weeks are continuing to be held around the country and the King sent £500 from the Duchy of Cornwall fund to help the village effort of Bradninch near Tiverton.

HERE IN BRITAIN

"The Wind in the Willows"

Mrs Kenneth Grahame presented the Bodleian with the holograph manuscript of her husband's famous book, together with the author's letters, written chapter by chapter as bedtime stories for his small son. Mr Grahame, who was secretary of the Bank of England, had to break off telling his bedtime stories when his son went away for seven weeks. The boy was loath to go as he would miss the stories of Mr Toad, but Grahame continued the stories nightly and posted them on for the whole of the holiday. The stories were read to the boy by his governess.

AROUND THE WORLD

"The Babies' Assembly Line"

Mother will drop her baby in the reception hall on her way into work. Baby will then be wheeled past a line of experts, who will examine his mouth and eyes, wash him, change his napkin and so on before passing him into the restaurant for feeding, on to a room for play and then into a cot for his nap, in an ever-moving, never-ending procession through a £250,000 streamlined nursery. This 'Victory Nursery' is the newest plan of Henry J Kaiser, record-breaking shipbuilder, being built to care for 1,500 babies of the mothers employed in his shipyards at Portland, Oregon.

Princess 'May' Of Teck

The Coronation of King George V

Queen Mary's coffin

The King's mother, Queen Mary, was 76 this week and celebrated her birthday by going to an Ensa concert in a village memorial hall dedicated to the memory of men of the village who fell in the last war. This was the most informal of all Royal Command Performances, for the stage was only 30ft wide and the audience had come by bicycle or walked through the woods. There were many soldiers in the hall, including those in the blue convalescent uniform, and the rest were villagers sitting on long forms in tight rows. In the centre of the front row was a red satin chair for the Queen.

Queen Mary was born Victoria Mary Augusta Louise Olga Pauline Claudine Agnes Mary in Kensington Palace in 1867 to Duke Francis and Duchess Mary of Teck. Young Mary, known as May, is the great-granddaughter of George III and a second cousin to Queen Victoria. At the behest of Queen Victoria, Mary was engaged to Queen Victoria's grandson Prince Albert Victor but he died shortly afterwards. Queen Victoria suggested that Mary marry Albert's brother George and although it was an arranged marriage, George and Mary fell deeply in love. When Queen Victoria died, Mary's father-in-law became King Edward VII and when he died, George became King George V and Mary was his Queen for 25 years. Her eldest son Edward became Edward VIII after the death of his father and on Edward's shocking abdication to marry Wallis Simpson, her second son, Albert, became our present King George VI.

The Dowager Queen Mary devotes herself to many charities, but also likes collecting jewels and she is known for wearing several dazzling pieces of jewellery all at one time. She might wear several necklaces, brooches, stomachers, bracelets, rings and of course a crown, often mixing diamonds, pearls, emeralds, sapphires and rubies.

IN THE NEWS

Friday 28   **"Wooden Soled Shoes"** It is probable that all ranges of men's footwear will become wooden soled. There is no tax on wood shoes which have been worn by factory workers for some time.

Saturday 29   **"No Bare Legs Please"** Bourne and Hollingsworth, the London west end store, banned its women going to work without stockings. *It is necessary for the highest standard of smartness to be maintained, otherwise efficiency is impaired. Compare the Civil Service where the staff smoke all day and dress how they like, with that of a uniformed service."*

Sunday 30   **"Bow Bells Signal Again"** The ban on the ringing of church bells having been lifted, the Bow bells have been reintroduced as the interval signal in BBC programmes.

Monday 31   **"One Result of Clothes Rationing"** In the two years that clothes rationing has been in operation, it is estimated that 500,000 tons of shipping space normally used for the importation of raw material and finished articles, have been made available for transporting troops and munitions.

Tuesday June 1 **"Mr Leslie Howard"** The 50-year-old distinguished film and stage actor is presumed to have lost his life while returning to this country by aeroplane from Lisbon.

Wednesday 2   **"King's Official Birthday"** The King's birthday falls on 14 December but was observed officially today. In the evening he took the Queen and Princesses Elizabeth and Margaret to see Arsenic and Old Lace at the Strand Theatre.

Thursday 3   **"Protection Against Diphtheria"** A new campaign to immunise 75% of the total child population of Britain against diphtheria was opened yesterday. In just two years, the Ministry has managed to get half the children of the country protected.

HERE IN BRITAIN
"Housewives to be Weighed"

The Ministry of Food has carefully studied the effects of rationing and changes in diet throughout the war and will now discover by regular, recorded checks whether people are gaining or losing weight.

The Ministry relies on scientific advisers for guidance on what is proper for keeping the nation fighting fit.. One way of doing this is to examine the trend of body weight and the survey now to be started will provide, at quarterly intervals, information of average weight in relation to height and age in various sections of the population.

AROUND THE WORLD
"Empire Day"

Empire Day, on 24 May, Queen Victoria's birthday, was celebrated throughout the Colonies with parades and services. The Secretary of State for the Colonies said sent the following message to the Colonial Empire.

"I send you on this Empire Day a message of confidence and good cheer. This last year has had its hardships, of which the people of the Colonial Empire have had their share, but it has also brought a steady improvement in our fortunes and prospects. We have still to pass-through many dangers and twe can now see more clearly the road to victory."

AVEBURY FOR THE NATION

Aerial laser scanning shows the huge bank and ditch surrounding the stones. The village of Avebury has grown across the site.

The National Trust has acquired 950 acres of land at Avebury which includes the greater part of the group of prehistoric remains that make this one of the most important archaeological sites of Europe. Some 300 acres have been bought from Mr Alexander Keiller FSA, who has carried out, at his own expense, valuable restoration work and discoveries since 1925. The Trust has, at the same time, bought Manor Farm, 650 acres which holds the other part of the Avebury Circles.

The National Trust has paid tribute to the generous way in which Mr Keiller has helped to secure this noteworthy addition to our national treasures. A public appeal for funds to meet the cost was considered impossible in wartime but happily, the Pilgrim Trust and Mr ID Margary, FSA came forward with substantial gifts.

People have used the Avebury landscape for many thousands of years, but the first people to farm crops and keep domesticated animals lived there from around 6,000 years ago. More than a thousand years later, at around 4,600 years ago, the bank and ditch were built, and soon after that, local stones were set up in at least three circles, surrounded by the bank and ditch which together form Avebury Henge. With its outer ring of massive stones enclosing over 28 acres and its bank, three-quarters of a mile in circumference, rising originally 50ft above the bottom of the ditch, it is the largest and most impressive work of its kind in all Europe.

Yet for centuries this revealing heritage was allowed to decay, when not actively ill-used. The megaliths have been treated as quarries for building-stone and in the Middle Ages many were buried. Even in the past month, Ordnance Survey have defaced two megaliths by chiselling in their Benchmarks

IN THE NEWS

Friday 4   **"Soft Fruits and Jam"** The manufacturers of jam will enjoy first claim to supplies of soft fruits, but if there are good crops some will be sold to the public through the shops.

Saturday 5   **"Save Salvage, Save Lives"** *'Would you save the life of a merchant seaman or a naval man if you could? Of course you would, but you are wasting men's lives each time you destroy a scrap of paper, throw waste food in the dustbin, or burn up rubbish that contains rags, metal, bones or rubber.'* A new salvage drive is *'your chance to form the salvage habit.'*

Sunday 6   **"London Calls for Telephonists"** Among the civilian jobs which women do, few are more important than the telephonist. Within the next 12 months the Post Office will require 2,000 more for London alone.

Monday 7   **"Petrol from Hold Pumped by Hand"** Merseyside firemen worked for two days in the hold of a 7,000-ton ship to pump out 1,500 gallons of high-octane aviation spirit which had leaked from damaged containers.

Tuesday 8   **"Newton's Birthplace for the Nation"** Thanks to the Royal Society and the Pilgrim Trust, Woolsthorpe Manor, near Grantham, the birthplace of Isaac Newton, is to be held by the National Trust.

Wednesday 9   **"Help for Farmers' Wives"** Domestic work on farmhouses may now, in cases where hours interfere with work on the farm, be an 'approved' category for war work and farmers' wives will be given domestic help.

Thursday 10   **"Stay at Home this Whitsun"** Travel restrictions will come into force tomorrow which mean that, for the Bank Holiday weekend, there will be no more long-distance trains than the number run ordinarily in May, nor will there be any extra buses.

HERE IN BRITAIN
"Nun Wins Epsom Derby"

A nun has won the Epsom "Derby". Not the real Derby, but a race run in aid of Epsom and Ewell's 'Wings for Victory' week. Mother Veronica who runs a riding school for children, entered the horse 'Saudades' as a million to one chance. He is only a hack and the children's pet but ridden by former real Derby winner, E Smith, the horse beat several thoroughbreds. There were other famous jockeys in the race too, Gordon Richards included. Mother Veronica was very surprised but said, "Saudades will remain the children's pet, we will never enter him for another race."

AROUND THE WORLD
"Russians Love of Flowers"

Russia is being swept by a craze for flowers and the flower-sellers in the Moscow streets are doing a roaring trade. Generals and children, tram drivers and sentries, all carry flowers.

Part of the Leningrad highway is patrolled by women guards who work with sprigs of lilac tucked in their belts beside their revolver holsters and those off duty have garlands of flowers round their forage caps.

They all know that there will again be no country holidays this summer and that the present light heartedness is likely to be short-lived.

DIG FOR VICTORY

In October 1939, the British Ministry of Agriculture launched the 'Dig for Victory' campaign. Food was 'a munition of war' and with shipping space at a premium for the war effort and imports hit hard by the attacks on shipping convoys, in this time of rationing, people across the country were encouraged to grow their own food in their gardens and allotments. Keeping people fed at a time of food shortages and maintaining national morale were key goals for this propaganda campaign, which resulted in the creation of 3.5 million allotments in Britain by 1943.

The severe shortage of imported wheat meant that the Ministry of Food were desperate to have not only the Army, but also the civilian population, eat potatoes instead of bread. The undoubted star of the 'Dig for Victory' campaign was 'Potato Pete'. Along with 'Doctor Carrot', he lent a jovial image to the entire enterprise – and gained something of a cult following, with songs celebrating his efforts becoming popular.

On the commercial side, professional horticulture was equally important and this month, at a meeting of the Farmers' Club, the lack of qualified personnel and first-class research programmes was discussed. The Secretary said in his address, *"Horticulture has never received the acknowledgement to which it is entitled, and even to-day, when much prominence is given to farming activities, little is heard of the horticultural section's contribution to the national effort."* The time is opportune to give serious consideration to obtaining vegetables in greater variety and an increased acreage of those which could be served alone, so that the housewife might have an easier task in furnishing an attractive daily menu. If it is found necessary to make a further reduction in the meat ration the public will be still more dependent on vegetables. A first-class research station for vegetables is needed.

JUNE 11ᵀᴴ - 17ᵀᴴ 1943

IN THE NEWS

Friday 11   **"Boating Ban Lifted"** Boating is allowed on the Norfolk Broads this Whitsun for the first time in two years. However, all motor-boats have been laid up since 1941.

Saturday 12   **"Aquarium Open for Whitsun"** London Zoo Aquarium has reopened in time for Whitsun. It has been closed since the beginning of the war.

Sunday 13   **"Children as Harvesters"** Teachers are protesting about the 'exploitation' of children called to help with the harvest. *'No child should work in potato fields for more than four hours a day and for a child to earn 35s to £2 a week is a dangerous economic experiment.'*

Monday 14   **"Quiet Whit Monday"** Most main-line railways were quiet as were the roads round London. Nevertheless, the police were out stopping motorists and checking they were not making unauthorised use of petrol.

Tuesday 15   **"Dead Soldiers' Pay"** Claims for the return of pay and allowances issued after the death of single servicemen have caused a good deal of bad feeling and anguish for parents.

Wednesday 16   **"WVS Fifth Birthday"** Over a million women are now members of the WVS who apply the 'principles of good housekeeping' to help run their country in its hour of need.

"Scarcity of Shoe Leather" The Ministry of Supply has stated that the country is facing a period of real shortages for the footwear industry and people should refrain from purchasing shoes they can do without.

Thursday 17   **"Railings Salved"** The Ministry of Works have confirmed that they have taken 580,000 tons of iron railings and 400,000 tons have already been converted to war purposes including bombs, tanks and ships.

HERE IN BRITAIN

"Praise for the WVS"

The Home Secretary paid a tribute to the Women's Voluntary Service on its fifth birthday. Initially formed to help recruit women into the Air Raid Precautions (ARP) movement, assisting civilians during and after air raids by providing emergency rest centres, feeding, first aid and assisting with the evacuation of children, their million volunteers are now involved in almost every aspect of wartime life from the collection of salvage to the knitting of socks and gloves for merchant seamen. A very long list of awards for outstanding service included five George Medals and 78 Empire awards.

AROUND THE WORLD

"'Zoot Suits' Cause Affray"

Los Angeles has been declared out of bounds for men in the US Navy, to stop them fighting with gangs of youths garbed in 'zoot suits' who, they assert, had robbed and beaten them and 'offered indignities to their women friends'. The Zoot Suit rioters who target servicemen and the police, are young Latinos and other minorities who wear baggy trousers with cuffs carefully tapered to prevent tripping; long jackets with heavily padded shoulders and wide lapels; and hats ranging from pork pies and fedoras to broad-brimmed sombreros. The violence is more about racial tension than fashion.

HONOURING THE FLAGS

United Nations Day was celebrated with the ceremony of honouring the flags in London, Cardiff and Edinburgh, with similar ceremonies in the USA and many parts of the Empire. In London there was a salute to the flags at the Duke of York's Steps in the Mall following a ceremonial march past. Before the arrival of the parade, the Scots Guards, carrying the 27 flags of the United Nations, took up position opposite the saluting dais and the band of the Coldstream Guards played during the march past.

Crowds packed the pavements to watch the parade headed by the Civil Defence services and the women's services - WRNS, ATS and WAAF, Queen Alexandra's Royal Naval Nursing Service and Queen Alexandra's Imperial Military Nursing Service. They were followed by a large contingent of war workers, including cotton spinners and weavers from Lancashire, wool textile operatives from Yorkshire, iron-ore miners and iron and steel workers from Northamptonshire, coalminers from Kent, land girls and the timber corps. The brown, blue and white overalls and dungarees of the workers, with the green jerseys and brown breeches of the land girls, added a further dash of colour to the display. This reminder of the important and vital work carried on in the factories and fields earned an especially warm cheer.

Then came the Merchant Navy and the Royal Navy, with a coloured bearded naval reserve officer in high leg boots recalling that the Dominions and colonies have units at sea as well as in the air and on the land. They were followed by the Royal Marines and the Royal Air Force contingent and the Dominion and Indian forces, whose columns were headed by flag-bearers carrying the flags of Canada, Australia, New Zealand, South Africa, India, Newfoundland, Southern Rhodesia and Burma. The Home Guard and units of the British Army wound up the procession.

JUNE 18TH - 24TH 1943

IN THE NEWS

Friday 18   **"The King in North Africa"** The King arrived in Morocco last Saturday since when he has visited British and US Warships followed by a tour of French forces which delighted the public.

Saturday 19   **"The New Viceroy"** Field Marshal Sir Archibald Wavell is to be the new Viceroy of India in the autumn. Lady Wavell, who as Vicereine of India will be virtually Queen to 400,000,000 people, is one of the least publicised of famous men's wives!

Sunday 20   **"Clothing for Occupied Europe"** The Hosiery and Knitwear Export Group is holding an exhibition of more than 300 items of British knitted underwear and other garments designed for people in enemy-occupied countries immediately they are liberated.

Monday 21   **"For a Better Life"** The Minister of Pensions, whose motto is 'Money payment is not enough' opened, on the outskirts of Liverpool, the first north-west occupational therapy centre for the rehabilitation of wounded, sick or pensioned soldiers.

Tuesday 22   **"Knights in Armour"** All crews of American heavy bombers will soon be going into battle clad in protective armour. 16 lb sleeveless vests of manganese steel, called 'flak waistcoats' have already been proved to be highly successful.

Wednesday 23   **"Queen Pins VC on 'Dam Buster'"** For the first time since the reign of Queen Victoria, a Buckingham Palace Investiture has been held by a Queen.

Thursday 24   **"Plans for Farm Cottages"** To ensure completion on time for the building of 3,000 agricultural cottages, the designs used are for an emergency. The cottages will satisfy a war-time standard and are not a model of a post-war agricultural cottage. Non-parlour types of houses will be let for 8s 6d (43p) a week and parlour types at 10s (50p).

HERE IN BRITAIN
"Microscopic Negatives"

A quarter of a million documents a week can be handled by the War Office microgram service. Microscopic negatives of documents are made abroad and then sent home by air. Documents formerly sent by rail and sea, now take only as many days to be dealt with as they previously took months. One hundred feet of film can hold as many as 1,600 documents in a container which is no bigger than a two-ounce tobacco tin. On arrival at the War Office the films are unpacked and put through a micro-printer, which develops at the rate of 1,000 documents an hour.

AROUND THE WORLD
"Charlie and the Glamour Girl"

Thrice wed Charlie Chaplin, the 54 year old London born comedian has eloped with his drama protégé, 18 year old Oona O'Neill, New York's No 1 Glamour girl of 1942. They married in California and his former protégé, Joan Barry, who claims he is the father of her unborn child, collapsed on hearing the news. Chaplin has denied paternity but has offered to pay for Miss Barry's medical and other expenses until the baby can be blood-tested. Oona, giving evidence in the paternity suit, said, *"Charles is a wonderful teacher, but I must say our relations have been strictly esoteric".*

THE PROMENADE CONCERTS

This week Sir Henry Wood begins his forty-ninth series of, BBC sponsored, Promenade Concerts. There have now been Promenade Concerts – literally, concerts where you can walk about, in London, for more than a hundred years and our present series can reasonably trace its ancestry to the entertainments in the public gardens of Vauxhall, Ranelagh and Marylebone in the eighteenth century. The original English promenade concerts at the Lyceum Theatre in 1838 were conducted by Musard and consisted of instrumental music of a light character, containing overtures, solos for a wind instrument and dance music (quadrilles and waltzes).

The change from theatre to concert hall, Queen's Hall, was made by Robert Newman when, in 1895, he started the present series with Henry J Wood as conductor. Newman wished to generate a wider audience for concert hall music by offering low ticket prices and an informal atmosphere, where eating, drinking and smoking were allowed. He said, *"I am going to run nightly concerts and train the public by easy stages. Popular at first, gradually raising the standard until I have created a public for classical and modern music."*

In 1927, the BBC saw that taking the concerts on would provide a full season for broadcast and would fulfil the Corporation's remit to 'inform, educate and entertain'. After the Queen's Hall was bombed in 1941 the Proms moved to the Albert Hall where their policy remains, classics plus new works and among the established artists, promising newcomers. This season contains 25 new works to be performed. Expectation is high for a new symphony by Dr Vaughan Williams and works for piano and orchestra by Britten, Moeran and Rubbra are prominent among the English contribution. The Dominions, the United States and the USSR have sent scores which will showcase modern music on both sides of the world.

IN THE NEWS

Friday 25 "The Stalingrad Sword" The King has approved the design for this sword of honour. It will be inscribed on one side: *"To the steel hearted citizens of Stalingrad the gift of King George VI, in token of the homage of the British people".*

Saturday 26 "Raise Canteen Standards" About a quarter of the total working population of Britain eat their midday meals every day in industrial canteens. The Ministry of Food wants the standard of meals to be raised.

Sunday 27 "Holiday Town Backs Bus Curfew" Brighton is saving 30,000 tons of petrol a year, ten tons of coal a month and about two million tyre miles a year since imposing a curfew.

Monday 28 "Considerate PO Service" At the Army Post Office, every complaint is investigated and receives a courteous, factual reply. The officer in charge admits there *are* sometimes delays, he does not take the view that 'the customer is always right'.

Tuesday 29 "London Passenger Transport" This month the LPT Board completes the first decade of its existence. It acquired and has maintained and extended the underground railways and the road passenger transport of an area of nearly 2,000 square miles.

Wednesday 30 "Morality and Venereal Disease" The Minister of Health said that the main factor in the present huge increase in syphilis, is the collapse of moral standards in parts of the population and an increase in promiscuity.

Thursday July 1 "Help – Make Jam" The Minister of Food has called on the Women's Institutes to help with the annual jam making. It is more necessary than ever to reduce, by every pound of jam we can make here, the import of fruit pulp from abroad.

HERE IN BRITAIN

"Torpedoing 'Monte Carlo Casino'"

A young officer in command of a British submarine in the Mediterranean is known now as *'the man who torpedoed the bank at Monte Carlo.'* He was recently on patrol off the French Riviera when he sighted an enemy vessel. His torpedoes quickly finished her off and the next day he sighted another enemy ship which was also sunk.

But he was pretty close in shore and two of his torpedoes missed, exploding with a roar just under the Monte Carlo Casino. 'Not a bad show,' one of his brother officers said, 'two enemy ships and a bank broken.'

AROUND THE WORLD

"Left Right, Left Right"

When there was an acute shortage of boots, a Dublin firm agreed to buy from a Manchester firm, 500,000 second-hand army boots at 6d (3p) a pair. One consignment contained 5,650 left-foot boots only, and it was stated that for some unaccountable reason right-foot boots wear out first in the army.

"Girl Gazing is no Crime"

In New York, a policeman charged a man for walking around Central Park staring at girls. The Judge told the officer, *"It's lucky you don't follow me around. If looking at women is a crime, there are lots of criminals on the street of New York and I'm one of them."*

THE PILGRIM TRUST

The Pilgrim Trust's first project was the shoring up of Durham Cathedral.

MEN WITHOUT
WORK

A Report made to the Pilgrim Trust

WITH AN
Introduction by the
ARCHBISHOP OF YORK
and a Preface by
LORD MACMILLAN

CAMBRIDGE
AT THE UNIVERSITY PRESS
1938

A few weeks ago, this Trust bought a collection of 858 books which once belonged to Sir Isaac Newton and have offered them to his old college, Trinity College, Cambridge. In the past few months, the Trust has made several significant grants to enable the National Trust to purchase properties for the nation.

The Pilgrim Trust was set up in 1930 by Edward Harkness, an American philanthropist, whose family traced its roots to Dumfriesshire. He retained a lifelong love of Great Britain and after the UK's contribution to the First World War, donated £2 million to create the Trust wanting it to support the urgent future needs of the UK. This large gift captured the country's imagination, and the King and Queen received him and his wife at Buckingham Palace. In 1931, the Trust's first grant of £25,000 went to Durham Castle, which with shifting foundations, was in urgent need of work to save the building from sliding into the River Wear but much of their early work has focused on the high levels of unemployment in the country and giving individuals work and volunteering opportunities.

The report they commissioned, 'Men Without Work', was a significant piece of research on the subject of unemployment and the needs of the unemployed, designed to provide the Pilgrim Trustees with guidance on the allocation of funding in relation to the social problems associated with unemployment. It explored who was unemployed and why across six towns.

At the outbreak of this War, an ambitious scheme was set up to employ artists on the home front. This was the brainchild of Sir Kenneth Clark working together with the Pilgrim Trust. The result is a collection of more than 1,500 watercolours and drawings that make up a fascinating record of British lives and landscapes at a time of imminent change.

JULY 2ND - 8TH 1943

IN THE NEWS

Friday 2   **"Silenced Sirens"** You may not hear them so often. The *vastly improved* warning system announced in Parliament does not involve a different method of warning the public but is a plan for confining Alerts to the areas affected.

Saturday 3   **"No Tube Tyres"** Experiments being made in Britain may revolutionise motoring by abolishing inner tubes for light cars. Most importantly, it will save rubber.

Sunday 4   **"War Factories Cover 3sq Miles"** Our new Ordnance factories are so big that some have as many as 700 or 800 separate buildings, with twenty miles of roads, railway stations and lines, and hostels for thousands of workers.

Monday 5   **"Glider Crosses the Atlantic"** A fully laden glider has been successfully towed across the Atlantic by a transport aircraft for the first time. The 3,500 miles from Montreal was accomplished in a flying time of 28 hours.

Tuesday 6   **"Sheepskins Aid the Bombers"** Sheep pelts, the skin left when all the wool is removed, can now be used as petrol filters on bombers. Before the war the pelts were processed as chamois leather dusters only, but now they are used as pocket linings, linings for ammunition boxes, flying helmets and linings for delicate instrument cases.

Wednesday 7   **"Unborn Babies Rations"** Expectant mothers will be entitled to additional milk a week, two shell eggs at each allocation, a ration and a half of meat, oranges as they are available and an orange juice and cod liver oil compound.

Thursday 8   **"Malta Home Rule"** Acknowledging the steadfastness and fortitude of the people of Malta, the Government propose after the war to restore responsible government to the island in the sphere of internal affairs.

HERE IN BRITAIN
"Missing Lion Comes Home"

After six months, two British lions from the Trowbridge (Wiltshire)Town Hall, have been reunited. However, it is just as much a mystery how the lion returned as to how he disappeared. Standing 3ft high and weighing nearly 1 cwt a piece, the two had sat at the end of the Town Hall's oak staircase for fifty-four years. Then one night, after a dance, one had vanished. The Council offered a £10 reward and the police were called, but to no avail. At 6 o'clock one morning this week, the Town Hall doorbell rang and when the caretaker opened the door, there, alone, was the lost lion.

AROUND THE WORLD
"Fourth of July"

Independence Day was celebrated by American troops in this country. There was a special service in St Paul's Cathedral, with a simultaneous broadcast from Washington Cathedral. Many American soldiers celebrated the day by entertaining, to lunch or dinner, British families who have acted as their hosts since their arrival in this country. In addition, there were picnics in Hyde Park and a river excursion to Windsor, where American seamen were received by the King and Queen and shown private rooms in the Castle before they began a tour conducted by official guides.

GLIDER CROSSES ATLANTIC

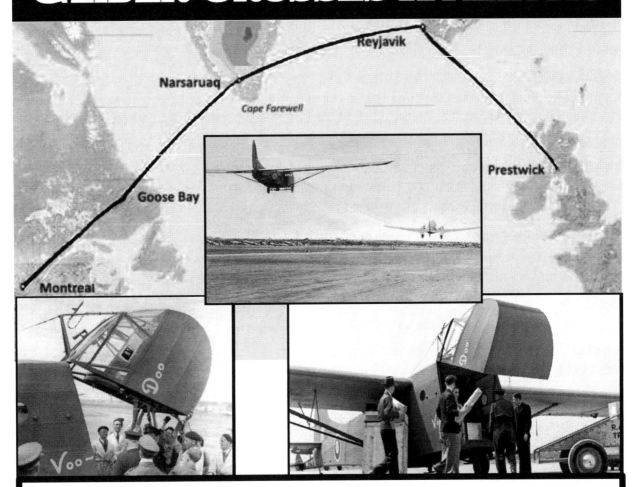

This week, a fully laden glider was towed across the Atlantic by RAF Transport Command. The idea of a transatlantic air freighter 'train' was conceived by Air Chief Marshal Sir Frederick Bowhill, of RAF Transport Command, who, while in charge of the North and South Atlantic Bomber Ferry from Canada, started experiments on the ultimate possibility of an Atlantic glider service for freight purposes. The glider, which has a wingspan of 84ft, was designed in the US and was fully laden with a ton and a half of war cargo including vaccines for Russia, radio, aircraft and motor parts, was towed by a Dakota, a twin-engine American aircraft.

On the journey from Montreal to Britain, weather conditions were mainly favourable, except that in the early stages a head wind made progress slow. After three hours flying the 'train' had reached a height of about 5,000ft trying to get above the clouds. When even at 13,000ft, the cloud bank towered above their heads, the pilots decided to descend and fly through the cloud instead. During the next three hours they came up against thunderstorms, ice and snow and the flyers were forced down to only 1,500 feet above ground. The trip was made in stages, with the glider reaching Britain exactly at the estimated time of arrival.

When the glider broke cloud over its destination, the towing aircraft was not visible, and it had the sky to itself whilst an interested group of spectators watched it make a perfect landing in the centre of the runway. Then the tug broke cloud, circled and dropped the towrope neatly at the appointed place, where an airman collected it - £80 worth of nylon. The tug landed and taxied to its station where a tractor delivered the glider alongside and within a few minutes the glider was unloaded.

JULY 9TH - 15TH 1943

IN THE NEWS

Friday 9 — **"23,000ft Delayed Drop"** A young RAF pilot from New Zealand has made an involuntary parachute descent which is a new world record for a delayed drop. Stunned and partly blinded when his plane went into an uncontrollable spin in a monsoon storm over Burma he fell 20,000ft with his parachute unopened, 3,000ft more than the previous record.

Saturday 10 — **"Civil Servants Sit-Down Strike"** 500 men and women working in the Ministry of Health, evacuated to Blackpool, sat down on the promenade tramlines to protest against being unable to get seats on the trains. Every tram was loaded with holidaymakers.

Sunday 11 — **"Remembrance Day for Seamen"** Services were held in churches throughout the country to observe a day of remembrance of the work of the Royal Navy and the Merchant Navy.

Monday 12 — **"New Road Menace"** With the huge demand for second hand cycles high prices are being charged by unscrupulous dealers selling unsafe machines. Recent accidents have been due to wheels collapsing, frames breaking, brakes failing and handlebars fracturing.

Tuesday 13 — **"Monty Slips Home"** It can now be stated that General Montgomery, Commander of the British Forces in Sicily, spent a fortnight in England in May. In spite of the secrecy of his trip, he received a tremendous welcome wherever he went!

Wednesday 14 — **"Blind Factory Workers"** During the last 12 months, over 700 blind men and women have been put in 80 occupations formerly done by sighted workers, with a negligible risk of injury.

Thursday 15 — **"Fewer Chocolates, More Sweets"** For children between seven and fourteen the total allocation will remain unaltered but as considerable supplies of chocolate are being sent to children in occupied Europe, there will be more vitamin enhanced sweets

HERE IN BRITAIN

"Bastille Day in Britain ..."

The fourth Quatorze Juillet spent in exile since the Germans marched into Paris was bravely celebrated by the Fighting French. At Wellington Barracks they held a 'prises d'armes' which, whatever the setting, exemplifies so well the French military spirit. There were the same trim, blue-clad detachments of chasseurs-à-pied, the familiar red pompoms of the naval contingent and a strong muster of French airmen looking as they always did in dark blue; there were the same martial airs, the same colours and pennants, but also there were hard-trained parachute troops and commandos in the battle-dress and green berets of their British comrades.

AROUND THE WORLD

" ...and in Algeria"

In Algiers, patriotic fervour was released in a Fourteenth of July demonstration such as the town has never seen when 200,000 people crowded the streets to witness the celebrations. General de Gaulle reviewed guards of honour of French, British and American troops where the three national anthems were played and then reviewed a military parade from a dais sporting a banner bearing the words 'Alger capitale de l'Empire.' An American band led detachments of American and British troops and then came the French detachment, appearing for the first time ceremonially in new drill uniforms modelled on the American uniform.

THE BOYS' CLUBS

*A south coast club outing.
The landing craft has been loaded and the
boys, and a few girls, are ready for the off.
A Royal Marine supervises.*

There has been a net increase over the past year in affiliated clubs amounting to the remarkable figure of 292, and the increase in members to 37,187, is a clear sign of the virility and strength of the Boys' Club movement but, said, Lord Aberdare, President of the National Association, at the annual conference, *"In the next two or three years the movement would have to play a critical innings. There might be need for decisiveness, determination, and courage."* Any weakness of the club movement in the eyes of the public in the years that lay ahead would, in his view, rob the nation of something that it would greatly need. Boy's Clubs are training boys to be 'fit' men, fit not just physically but spiritually and intellectually, through a concern for play, comradeship and self-government, and there must be the strength of 'fit' manhood in their leadership.

Lord Aberdare told the delegates a great revolution was taking place and we could never go back. The country was, perhaps, passing through the greatest period in our history and entering a new age where it seemed to be accepted that society would to a larger extent than before, be a planned society. But if freedom is denied in one sphere, it should be secured elsewhere. If after the war, he said, our industrial and economic life and education is to be largely planned, then leisure life must be the place for the exercise of real freedom. *'To put it in practical terms, the club must show the boy the joy of that coordination of hand and eye which made a perfect stroke at cricket, the sheer physical satisfaction which came from a hard-fought game, the creative satisfactions of arts and crafts, and the intellectual satisfactions of drama and literature.'*

JULY 16TH - 22ND 1943

IN THE NEWS

Friday 16 **"Utility Braces"** Men's braces which have been scarce and high priced, will be available in Utility styles. Made of leather and webbing, they will be cheap. Boys' size 1s ¾d (5p) and adults' range 1s 1¼d (5p) to 3s 6d (17p).

Saturday 17 **"King's Visit to Canadian Camp"** The King and Queen visited a Canadian Army camp in England and the King made the first presentation of Colours to the Royal Regiment of Canada and the South Saskatchewan Regiment.

Sunday 18 **"Vitamins in War Factories"** Supplies of orange juice, cod liver oil compound and vitamins A and D will be available where any married women spend much of their time, full or part time, in a war factory.

Monday 19 **"Hansard Title Revived"** After fifty-four years the Official Report of Parliamentary debates is to revert to its old name of Hansard. In 1800 William Cobbett issued Cobbett's Parliamentary Debates. These were printed by Thomas Hansard.

Tuesday 20 **"Bucket and Spade Wanted"** The shortage of children's seaside spades and buckets has led to a ramp in the price of wooden spoons, cake tins and enamel pudding basins which the children are using as substitutes.

Wednesday 21 **"Airport, Land and Sea Terminals"** Plans for a £20,000,000 combined land plane and flying-boat airport for London have been put forward by a designer with a selected site on the Thames Estuary, a few miles east of Gravesend, in mind.

Thursday 22 **"Mr Bevin's Warning for Boys"** The Minister of Labour has emphasised the serious shortage of manpower in the coal industry and said he would have to resort to some desperate remedies during the coming year. *'I shall have to direct young men to the coal industry.'*

HERE IN BRITAIN

"Triumph of Organising"

A firm which before the war made vehicles for roads and railways has become, in three years, the centre of a group of factories building the latest type of Halifax bomber. There are eight factories in the group all of which were motor vehicle makers or motor body builders before joining forces. Not more than one in eight of the work people of the group had ever been employed in an engineering factory and half the total labour force is female. Women are used in all departments and to a remarkably large extent on the final erection of the aircraft.

AROUND THE WORLD

"1,475 Mile Oil Pipe Line"

The oil pipeline, which has been built across nine States from the Texas oil fields to the eastern seaboard in 350 days, has been opened. The line, which cost $95M to build will bring 12.6M gallons of petroleum daily to east coast refineries.

A second pipeline will be soon added. The decision to build these lines was made when Axis submarine attacks in the western Atlantic, directed principally at tankers, was at its height. That menace has since ended but the pipeline will release tankers for the transatlantic service.

MORE BABIES PLEASE!

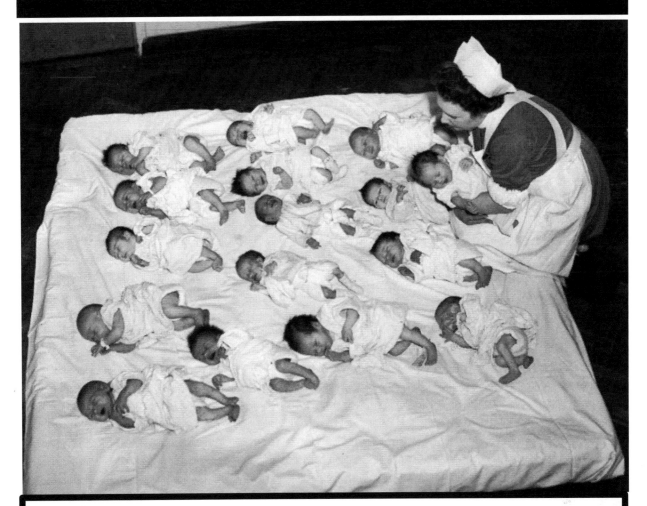

The MP who opened a debate in the House of Commons on the causes of the decline in the birth-rate - apart from the upward trend during the present war - and the danger of this tendency if unchecked, pointed out that decline in population went hand in hand with improved material conditions. He urged that an example to parents to have larger families ought to be shown by those at the top of the social scale and his proposals for encouraging larger families included family allowances, which the Government had accepted in principle, and the provision of houses with labour-saving devices to accommodate families. He also called for a stop to the refusal of landlords to let their houses to parents with children. There was general agreement that the financial measures to encourage larger families were not of themselves enough and there should be a raising of the status of motherhood. Labour MP, Dr Summerskill , was specific. *"The mother must be given a legal right to a share in the family income,"* she said, *"the woman would then have the dignity and status of a partner instead of the everlasting humiliation of a dependent."*

The Government is to set up an inquiry and reasons already put forward in the debate included: Fear of war and insecurity, standards of life, maternal mortality, lack of pre-natal care and advice, housing – babies and apartments do not go together happily - and the desire for women to have careers. During the war, hundreds of women have gone into industry for the first time, whether single or married, and enjoyed an income of their own and begun to enjoy economic independence. The last laugh came from an MP who said, *"There must be control over the sale of Conservatives – I mean, contraceptives!"*

July 23rd - 29th 1943

IN THE NEWS

Friday 23   "**Excellent Dried Foods**" The Minister of Food is planning the erection of thirty factories for the dehydration of fresh cabbages, carrots and potatoes, as far as possible, in the vegetable growing districts. The whole output, government property, will be required to meet the demands of the Armed Forces.

Saturday 24   "**Women in Revolt**" Thousands of women engineers are involved in a wages dispute in a Scottish factory where there is interchange of jobs between men and women. The men are paid the appropriate rate – the women, approximately half.

Sunday 25   "**Mussolini Resigned**" The King of Italy has assumed supreme command of the Italian armed forces and Marshal Badoglio is the new Prime Minister. But the war goes on.

Monday 26   "**Soya in Sausages**" The war-time sausage will be less mystifying and more satisfying, if not meatier. It will now be composed as to 37% meat with the balance being made up of soya and filler of National flour and water plus seasoning or flavouring. This will be enforced by the Ministry of Food, which is distributing supplies of soya for the purpose.

Tuesday 27   "**Harmless Stains**" The council at Yoxford in Suffolk has put a sort of colour bar on their local river. They have dyed the water an unpleasant brown to deter bathers. The sewage from the village runs into the river and there is a risk of a diphtheria epidemic.

Wednesday 28   "**The Churchills Go to the Zoo**" Mr and Mrs Churchill went to London Zoo to see the four lion cubs of which Mr Churchill's lion 'Rota' is the father. The African lion was presented to the Prime Minister in February.

Thursday 29   "**Flying Boat Crash**" Ten occupants of a British Overseas Airways flying boat were killed and fifteen other injured when the aircraft crashed into a mountain in fog and burst into flames in a lonely part of County Kerry.

ONLY HERE
"A Paper …"

A correspondent of The Times has written to inquire if the Ministry of Supply ever received the instruction *"to save everybody's time by condensing official papers and avoiding official jargon".* He was driven to ask the question by the receipt this week of a 'Special Direction' made under the Control of Paper (No. 48) Order, 1942, which had come to him from the Deputy Controller of Paper for the Minister of Supply. **Here is the first Paragraph:** *Notwithstanding anything contained in the Control of Paper (No. 48) Order, 1942, Directions Nos. 6 and 7, the Minister of Supply hereby directs in lieu of the provisions thereof that you shall not (subject to the provisions hereinafter contained) …*

IN BRITAIN
"… Consumption Puzzle"

… consume in the period 27th June, 1943, to the 30th October, 1943, in the production of the news-bulletins, magazines or periodicals mentioned in the first column of the schedule to the Special Direction (hereinafter referred-to as the previous Direction) issued under the Control of Paper (No. 48) Order, 1942, tinder Control Reference 166/43, a quantity of paper (including any paper printed or made outside the United Kingdom) the aggregate weight of which exceeds the weight set out opposite that news-bulletin, magazine or periodical in the second column of that schedule plus one-seventeenth thereof."

WOMEN'S LAND ARMY

The Minister of Food, after watching a march past of hundreds of East Suffolk members of the Women's Land Army, said he could confirm the opinion of the American woman who, after returning home, said *'her outstanding impression was the endurance, patience and fortitude of British women'*. The Minister said, *'The Land Army is the fourth defence service of the country.'*

In 1938, Lady Denman was approached to re-form the Women's Land Army and in 1939, recruitment began in earnest. The Land Army girls are a mobile force of women ready to undertake all kinds of farm work in any part of the country. They wear their distinctive uniform and are normally employed and paid by the individual farmers, but the organisation supervises their lodging arrangement and their general welfare. Replacing male farm workers who have gone to war, the women come from all walks of life and despite having little or no agricultural experience, they are found ploughing fields, growing the produce, milking the cows, catching the rats, driving the tractors and much, much more.

There is also an 'army' of women who, unable because of domestic commitments to travel or live away, offer their services for work in their home district, and all on minimum wage. In 1941, *'In the Event of Invasion'*, Land Girls were encouraged to stick to their jobs, but advice was also issued on how to disable tractors if in real danger of capture by the enemy. This year, members are producing the vast majority of our war time food.

This quotation from Lady Denman, the Director of the Women's Land Army, summarises the importance of the Land Girls. *'The land army fights in the fields. It is in the fields of Britain that the most critical battle of the present war may well be fought and won.'*

JULY 30TH - AUG 5TH 1943

IN THE NEWS

Friday 30   **"Call Up Changes"** Women up to the age of fifty are to be roped in for war work. Girls who could pass into one or other of the women's auxiliary services must now go into aircraft factories.

Saturday 31   **"Cheering the Troops"** ENSA are now forming two mobile columns of entertainment to go wherever the troops go. One has mobile cinemas and the other Live Entertainment.

Sun August 1   **"Exodus from London"** Although the public were informed there was no relaxation of railway travel restrictions this Bank Holiday, thousands of people bent on seeking a change of scene filled the main London stations.

Monday 2   **"Sport of Kings"** The King and Queen went to Ascot joining thousands of holiday-makers at the races. They appeared in the royal box to a great outburst of cheering.

Tuesday 3   **"Women's Day in the House"** Labour MP, Dr Summerskill, opened the barrage, *'It is rather curious'* she said *'there has not been a strong agitation yet for equal pay for women in the Services. The Minister of Labour recently told the country he was amazed, in industry, to find that one woman was often capable of greater output than two men.'*

Wednesday 4   **"A Charter for Midwives"** A report to the Minister of Health recommends, for the first time, national scales of salary for certified midwives and for them to have a recognised, protected uniform of their own.

Thursday 5   **"Shortage of Partners"** A 'rationing system' has been introduced in several north-west holiday towns for dance partners. Since the start of the holiday season there has been a great scarcity of men. At Blackpool there are ten women to one man.

HERE IN BRITAIN

"Queues for Work and Lodgers"

Amazing contrasts were seen around the country on this Bank Holiday. While at some seaside resorts crowded holidaymakers were queuing for something to eat and drink after sleeping all night in deck chairs on the prom, landladies at Blackpool were queuing up at the town's information bureau to ask for lodgers – and at one industrial town, holidaymakers were queuing up at a factory for work!

It was a canning factory in Sheffield where an urgent call had gone out for helpers to deal with a glut of plums which would have gone bad if left over the holiday.

AROUND THE WORLD

"China's President Dies"

President Lin Sen died last night at the age of 76. He began his career in 1932 as a political figurehead, but the 'grand old man' of China has gradually emerged as a patriarchal symbol of the State.

The unobtrusive, unassuming, bearded figure, in his familiar black cape and grey felt hat, came to be regarded by the people not with awe but with the deepest respect and veneration traditionally accorded to a man of learning and culture. General Chiang Kai- shek invariably insisted on walking a step behind the President whenever they appeared in public together.

UNDERGROUND HEROES

At the beginning of the war, the government was against people sheltering in the Underground tunnels during air raids. They feared that once people entered, they would be reluctant to come back above ground and continue normal life. More importantly, they were concerned that disease would spread due to the small number of toilets in some stations or that people would fall on the tube lines.

However, especially during the Blitz, when people began to force their way into the Underground stations and the arguments were proved wrong, the government changed its view and began kitting out some stations with bunks, first aid kits and chemical toilets. Night after night, just before the sirens sounded, thousands trooped down, taking their bedding with them, flasks of hot tea, snacks, radios, packs of cards and magazines. People had their regular places and set up little communities.

However, Underground stations are not completely safe as bomb shelters – they are still vulnerable to a direct hit and a high explosive bomb can penetrate up to fifty feet through solid ground. When a small bomb scored a direct hit on the Marble Arch subway, filled with people in September 1940, its blast ripped the white tiles off the walls and made them deadly projectiles killing twenty people.

The most destructive incident happened in October 1940 at Balham station when a 1400 kg fragmentation bomb fell on the road above the northern end of the platform tunnels, creating a large crater into which a double decker bus then crashed. The northbound platform tunnel partially collapsed and was filled with earth and water from the fractured water mains and sewers above. Although more than 400 managed to escape, 68 people died in the disaster. Many were drowned as water and sewage from burst mains poured in.

AUG 6TH - 12TH 1943

IN THE NEWS

Friday 6   **"Parliament Rises"** MPs dispersed for the summer recess - due back in late September but Parliament can be recalled at short notice – and members are expecting that.

Saturday 7   **"Women in Engineering"** A drive to place women workers in the engineering industry on a 100% trade union basis is being made by four of the UK's largest workers' organisations.

Sunday 8   **"Trilingual Boys"** Teachers of Speech and Drama are calling for a survey on the teaching of spoken English. One teacher declared many children had triple speech - one for use in school, one for the playground and one for the home. He asked one boy who spoke very nicely if he spoke like that at home. *'Oh no, if I did, they would tell me not to swank.'*

Monday 9   **"Gandhi's Year in Gaol"** A partial hartal (strike) and a few minor attempts at demonstrations occurred in Bombay on the anniversary of the arrest of Mr Gandhi, but they passed off quietly.

Tuesday 10   **"Mosquitoes Fly the Atlantic"** Deliveries of Mosquitoes built in the Canadian De Havilland factory have begun. The all-wooden Mosquito has shown itself to be one of the RAF's most versatile machines. It is the fastest bomber ever built and can outpace any enemy fighter.

Wednesday 11   **"WAAF Volunteers"** Vacancies for women pilots in Air Transport Auxiliary, the civilian organisation responsible for ferrying aircraft from the factories to RAF maintenance units and squadrons, are to be filled by volunteers from the WAAF.

Thursday 12   **"A Visit Widely Welcomed"** Mr Churchill's visit to Quebec has been welcomed with a 'quiet and deep pleasure' by people of all ranks in that country.

HERE IN BRITAIN
"Saving the Bacon"

For many years the Dunmow Flitch has been awarded to those couples who at the historic trials, could prove the happiness of their marriage. For the first recorded occasion since the trials began in the twelfth century, this year's winners have had to hand the bacon back. Instead of the customary flitches (sides of bacon), gammons were borrowed from the local stores, but rationing restrictions made it necessary for the gammons to be returned after the trials. The winners received token presentations only. After the two-hours' trial, the winning couples were chaired around Dunmow, preceded by Morris dancers.

AROUND THE WORLD
"A Love-Sick Elephant"

Argentine animal lovers are indignant at the shooting at Buenos Aires Zoo of Dalia, a male 60-year-old Indian elephant weighing five tons. Dalia's mate died some years ago and since then he has been inconsolable, his love sickness causing periodical attacks of madness. He was given another mate, Conga, a young African elephant, but either because she was too young for him or because her character didn't suit, Dalia did not reciprocate her love. In one of his recent rages Dalia became dangerous and refused to obey his keeper, began to break the bars of his cage and there was a risk that he might escape.

FLOATING THE NORMANDIE

The Normandie pre war

The Normandie as the USS Lafayette awaiting salvage in the Hudson River.

Since February last year, the USS Lafayette, formerly the French steamship Normandie, once the biggest and fastest liner afloat, has been a charred hulk lying capsized on her side at her Hudson River pier. Now, in one of the biggest salvage operations ever attempted, US Navy engineers have floated her. The ship was submerged with water and mud everywhere below the water line. First, all the superstructure that was not buried in mud was sheared off. Then work began inside the hull to make it watertight and scores of emergency bulkheads were built to withstand the strain when raising her. Divers had to work in total darkness in the muddy water and find their way through a maze of passages, state rooms and machinery spaces by memorising the ship's plans. It is estimated that the total cost of salvage, including pumping out 100,000 tons of water from the ship, will be $3,750,000.

The 1,000ft French SS Normandie cost $60,000,000 to build and was then the largest and fastest liner in the world, making her maiden voyage from Le Havre to New York in 1935 in just over four days. She was the height of luxury with most of her passengers travelling First Class, enjoying the luxuries of the grandest hotels. She boasted a swimming pool, dance floors, numerous bars and a dining room which had doors rising 20ft high. The SS Normandie made 139 crossings before she was confiscated by the Americans at the advent of World War Two and after Pearl Harbour was attacked by the Japanese, she was renamed USS Lafayette and was being converted into a troop ship. It was when this work was almost completed, that a spark from a welder's torch set fire to a bale of life jackets and the liner was destroyed in the blaze.

IN THE NEWS

Friday 13   **"Tea For 1944"** By buying up the 1943 tea crops from the British Empire - a total of more than 700M lb - the Ministry of Food has secured that next year's tea ration will be undiminished.

Saturday 14   **"End of Double Summertime"** Clocks go back an hour over night. The reversion to ordinary summertime brings a much earlier black-out. The black-out will begin half an hour after sunset instead of three quarters of an hour.

Sunday 15   **"Coupons Cut for Stockings"** Seamless rayon and cotton stockings for women and men's woollen socks will cost fewer 'points', 1½ coupons and 2 coupons respectively, but more points will be needed for shoes, other than utility types with wooden soles.

Monday 16   **"Home Craft Lessons for ATS Gun Girls"** Britain's ATS girls are answering the Queen's call to become home makers of the future. They are being taught how to do minor household repairs at a special 'handy-women's' school.

Tuesday 17   **"Record Wings for Victory"** The certified figures for all the Weeks show a total of £615,945,000 with 29.1% representing 'small savings.' Money from ordinary individuals.

Wednesday 18 **"National Fire Service"** Their second birthday was celebrated all over the country. In London a parade in Hyde Park was attended by representatives of all the fire forces in England and Wales.

Thursday 19   **"WRENS with Churchill"** More than thirty WREN officers from Britain are with the PM's party in Canada for specialist duties during the conference in Quebec. Some will then go on to Washington to relieve Wrens who have been there for two years.

HERE IN BRITAIN
"Storm After 93 Degrees"

News has just been released of one of the most remarkable thunder storms in the London district on the evening of July 31 when thousands of stay-at-home holidaymakers were caught in a downpour of torrential rain. The storm, which ended a six-day heat wave, was started by a gale of such violence that in some areas, gables were wrenched off houses. So much fruit was blown off the trees that London shops opened after the holidays with big supplies of plums and early apples. Gables and chimneypots were hurled from houses, windows were broken, and hundreds of trees blown down.

AROUND THE WORLD
"Leapfrogging Aero Car"

William Stout, a famous aircraft designer, has forecast for the post-war use of Americans, an aerocar which will travel along roads at 70mph and, contemptuous of traffic cops, soar into the sky at 100 mph. It will carry three passengers and weigh about 1,500lb, half as much as a light aircraft.

A propeller in the rear drives the vehicle whether on the road or in the air. To get the machine in the air, the driver would swing the detachable 35ft wings into place. He has also promised, for everyday use, a 'helicab', streamlined helicopter carrying two to five people.

But lucky for others! *'This well conducted patrol should be an encouragement to any commanding officer who is superstitious.'* So said the captain of a British submarine flotilla in the Mediterranean about his 13th patrol, which began on the 13th of the month, lasted 13 days and resulted in a successful attack on enemy ships. However, for many, Friday 13th which occurs one to three times per year is regarded as a most unlucky day. Superstitions surrounding the date are thought to originate in the middle-ages and there are dozens of fears, myths and old wives' tales associated with the date all over the world.

The number 13 and Friday both have an individual long history of bringing bad luck. In the Bible, Judas, who betrayed Jesus, was the 13th guest to sit down to the Last Supper. In Norse mythology, a dinner party of the gods was ruined by the 13th guest called Loki, 'god of deceit and evil', who caused the world to be plunged into darkness. Peoples of the Mediterranean, regarded 13 with suspicion, not being as perfect as 12, which is divisible in many ways.

As for 'Friday', according to tradition, Adam and Eve were expelled from Eden; Cain murdered Abel; St John the Baptist was beheaded and the enactment of the order of Herod for the massacre of the innocents, all took place on a Friday. In Chaucer's Canterbury Tales, written in the 14th Century, he says 'and on a Friday fell all this mischance'. Here in Britain, Friday was once known as 'Hangman's Day' because it was usually when people who had been condemned to death would be hanged and the great crash of 1869, when the price of gold plummeted, was on Friday too.

AUG 20TH - 26TH 1943

IN THE NEWS

Friday 20 **"Liverpool Dockers Go Back to Work"** Thousands of men have been on strike in support of 34 dockers suspended because they would not work until 9pm. These men are to be reinstated and their grievances investigated.

Saturday 21 **"Last Night of the Proms"** The Promenade Concerts ended with an all-British programme. Walton's 'Crown Imperial' March opened and Sir Henry Wood's, 'Fantasia on British Sea Songs' was the traditional ending.

Sunday 22 **"Refugee Gets Film Contract"** Seventeen-year-old Angela Lansbury, daughter of the British actress Moyna Macgill, has signed a film contract in Hollywood. Miss Lansbury went to the States three years ago as a refugee.

Monday 23 **"1m Volt X-Rays"** Two years of development has culminated in the production at the General Electric laboratories in America, of rays carrying the highest X-ray voltage ever attained.

Tuesday 24 **"Short Run for Tolstoy"** 'War and Peace' was withdrawn from the Phoenix Theatre, London, after a run of only twenty performances, as it has failed to attract the public.

Wednesday 25 **"Men for Coal Pits"** The National Union of Scottish Mineworkers have said that rather than youth labour, they feel strongly that the needs of the time could be best met by recalling miners called up to the army.

Thursday 26 **"Britain Now a Debtor Nation"** *'The country has passed from a creditor to a debtor nation and as such it is essential that she should have an expanding export market'*, declared the president of the US Chamber of Commerce. This could mean adjusting tariffs and the rules of International Trade.

HERE IN BRITAIN
"Daren't Leave Shoes Out"

Boot and shoe thefts from outside hotel bedroom doors have become so prevalent many guests are preferring to have them cleaned by a 'boot black'. *'American soldiers and sailors are our best customers,'* a Liverpool boot black said, *'but recently,'* he added, *'we have had many people who stay at hotels'*. Said one hotel manager, *'This type of hotel theft was practically unknown before clothes rationing was introduced. There is also at present an epidemic of thieving of ladies' clothes from the bedrooms, particularly silk stockings and expensive lingerie.'*

AROUND THE WORLD
"Presents for the United States"

The Coronation Scot, the famous British de-luxe train is among gifts to the US government from Britain, Canada, Cuba, Mexico, Venezuela, Brazil, Peru and other Central and South American countries as well as from every part of the US as well.
The train, which millions of Americans viewed at the New York World's Fair, is now in the service of the US Army. Other gifts include watches, bells, beans, beeswax, rubber, sugar, whisky, ambulances, aeroplanes, rifles, racing pigeons, German iron crosses, a sled complete with seven dog team and an antique shaving mug.

90

STEEL CITY CENTENARY

Making armaments in 1943 (above) with illustrations of the Sheffield steel and cutlery industry of 1843 (right and below).

This week saw the centenary of Sheffield's incorporation as a borough and whilst a huge celebration was thought inappropriate at this time, the City Council arranged an indoor pageant depicting the history of the civic progress and the life of their people. It was a spectacle of the last 100 years, but the history of Sheffield goes back much further, to the Roman legions and woven into the tapestry over the years were Mary Queen of Scots, held prisoner here for 14 years; Cardinal Wolsey, entertained here on his way to the Tower; great nobles like the de Furnivals, the Talbots and the Howards and the romantic figure of Robin Hood and his merry men who ranged the forests.

The history of the growth of the steel industry is central to the pageant. Bessemer, Mushet and Siemens taught the manufacturers of Sheffield how to make the finest steel and become the great producer it is today. In the early days, it had to face a reign of terror against masters who were unpopular and men who refused to join the newly formed industrial workers' societies. The ratteners (saboteurs) stole the tools used by the workers who would not join the unions and later bombs were used and houses blown up with gunpowder.

In 1861, the Atlas Steel works began rolling armour plates for iron-plated frigates but forty-three years ago Sheffield met the most formidable challenge in its industrial history when America produced a harder steel. Sheffield chemists found the answer and one of the first messages of congratulations this week, has come from the city of Pittsburgh. The pageant expresses great pride in Sheffield in being chosen to forge the sword of honour for Stalingrad, *'that far city where the tide of war beat for long months against a wall of steel and fell back broken.*

AUG 27TH - SEPT 2ND 1943

IN THE NEWS

Friday 27   **"Service in the Mines"** Men of any age, if called up, can now enlist for service in the mines with the same right to demobilisation they would have if they enlisted in one of the fighting services.

Saturday 28   **"Food Supplies for Attack"** The Minister said they were now planning for attack and any stocks of food he could accumulate would not be used to increase rations but be 'jealously guarded' for the great tasks ahead.

Sunday 29   **"Schools for Trawler Boys"** Special schools for budding trawler men or special courses for them in existing schools, are contemplated to encourage the best possible type of youngster. Up to the present time, there has been no system of apprenticeship

Monday 30   **"Miners Resume Sunday Work"** The Lancashire and Cheshire miners have lifted their ban on Sunday work and overtime which was costing the country 20,000 tons of coal a week.

Tuesday 31   **"Clothes Repair Racket"** Price control is being considered following widespread complaints that excessive prices are being charged for repairs. High prices are defeating the Government's 'Mend and Make Do' appeal.

Weds Sept 1   **"Coupons for Children with Big Feet"** Extra clothing coupons for young children unusually big for their ages or who take adult sizes in footwear will continue. Children will be weighed and measured at school during October.

Thursday 2   **"NAAFI Girls to Serve in Europe"** Volunteers have been called from the 40,000 NAAFI canteen girls willing to work abroad. Referring to a wide scale invasion of Europe, *"Those same men whom you have come to know will be in urgent need of rest, refreshment and a cheerful smile – your smile."*

HERE IN BRITAIN

"Enemy Spy Messages"

Relatives and friends of prisoners of war in Germany may have noticed peculiar markings on their letters. They are left from chemical tests made by the British censorship to frustrate attempts by the enemy to communicate with his agents. In the last war the German secret service tried this and it has attempted the same thing again. To frustrate these efforts, incoming and outgoing letters are subjected by the censorship in this country to a chemical test which discloses any writing in invisible ink. To get reports from their spies here, the Germans tell their agents to address their letters to British prisoners.

AROUND THE WORLD

"A Believer in Wine"

A Portuguese woman who has just celebrated her 94th birthday in her village near Sintra, has averaged for the past 80 years, two and a half litres of wine daily. She still does her own housework and walks more than a mile to church.

It is calculated that this enthusiastic apostle of the health benefits of the grape has consumed the equivalent of more than 70,000 bottles of red wine. Her other staple diet is bread and soup, but she always sleeps with a flagon of wine at her bedside in order to ward off the possible dangers of insomnia.

MAKING MORE FROM LESS

An exhibition by the Ministry of Supply, illustrates the ingenuity, resource and inventive skill which have been employed to make good the loss of oversea imports. Production has been trebled since 1940 although the import of raw materials has halved. New materials, new designs, and new methods of manufacture have all contributed to the result, necessity having proved the prolific mother of invention.

Some changes have been simple. A new design of cotton reel which saves 6,000 tons of wood a year; solid wood lapping boards used by drapers as a core for rolls of fabric are now a frame covered with paper saving 50,000 tons of wood a year; slats instead of solid seats in barrack room forms have saved 1,815,000 cu ft of timber.

In producing munitions, the electric forging of six-pounder armour-piercing shells entirely abolishes waste and for shells from 25-pounders to the 9.2 howitzers a new method of forging has saved 400,000 tons of steel and 18,000,000 man-hours of work. The recuperator block of a 25-pounder gun, when made of welded tubes, is 900lb lighter than the old solid forging. An auxiliary aircraft petrol tank to be jettisoned is being made of paper and landing wheel fairings for fighters of fibre. A new process for rifle barrels was not shown to save materials, but the manpower which formerly produced two now produces 100.

The new bayonet of fabricated parts saves 60% labour and 50% steel. Plastic is taking the place of metal in the nose caps of shells and 2,000 tons of brass a year are saved by making regimental badges and buttons of plastic. During the last year over 1,000,000 pairs of Army boots have been returned to service with a saving of 7s (35p) a pair, and because 'broken in' they are described as 'better than new.'

SEPT 3RD - 9TH 1943

IN THE NEWS

Friday 3   **"National Observance Day"** From small villages to big cities, in military camps and factories, in shops and harvest fields, there was a brief break for an act of worship on this fourth anniversary of Britain's entry into the war.

Saturday 4   **"Treatment Centre for Dockers"** A rehabilitation centre for dockworkers in Salford opened. Recovery from ailments which predominate absenteeism, sciatica, rheumatism and gastric trouble, together with neglected injuries, can be expedited here.

Sunday 5   **"Trivial Mishaps"** Most of the 8,000 deaths which occur every year through accidents in the home are caused by trivial things such as tripping over a piece of torn linoleum or being scalded by overturned kettles.

Monday 6   **"No Christmas Cards for Troops"** The Postmaster General regrets that circumstances will not permit the dispatch of these cards and censorship regulations will not therefore be relaxed as in former years to permit such greetings cards.

Tuesday 7   **"More Rail Bars"** So that passengers can obtain snacks to take with them on trains, a distinct 'compact' design of Rail Bar has been adopted by the LMS. The first is at Crewe and others are being opened at Preston, Derby, Sheffield, and Rugby.

Wednesday 8   **"First In, First Out"** Length of service in the Forces will be the key principle of the Government demobilisation plan which is now being worked out. Key men will not be demobbed before those who have fulfilled the longest service.

Thursday 9   **"Concentrator Plants"** Since May, collections of kitchen waste has increased from 12,000 tons a month to 34,000 tons. There are 44 concentrator plants and some 57 boiling plants in constant use, sterilising over 60% of the waste before sale.

HERE IN BRITAIN
"Hard Work with Stretchers"

RAMC orderlies and stretcher bearers must be fit to do stretcher work in the field. All training centres have the 'best assault course' and cadets go round the obstacles carrying a badly wounded man firmly strapped to a stretcher.

They pull him through tunnels with live ammunition going off; over tall walls and piles of loose wood; drop him down high cliffs and carry him back up again and take him through fire and smoke. Carrying a wounded man of average weight, with his full kit, over this obstacle course, needs perfect physical condition.

AROUND THE WORLD
"Famous Express Wrecked"

The US has suffered one of the worst disasters in this country's railway history. The famous Congressional Limited, running from Washington to New York, was derailed just north of Philadelphia at 6pm while travelling at 70 miles an hour. Eight of its 16 coaches were derailed and 79 people were killed. About 100 passengers were injured, many seriously. Burned-out housing for the end of an axle caused the axle to break as the train was rounding a curve in the track. This was at the front end of the seventh coach, which was thrown almost vertically into the air, dragging other coaches from the track.

RAF AIR PHOTOGRAPHY

A sequence of aerial reconnaissance photographs of Utah Beach (bottom) prior to the D-Day landings.

Since 1939, the RAF Photographic Reconnaissance Units had been providing the country with revealing pictures including aerial photos of bomb damage in Germany, Italy, and enemy-occupied territory. The specially trained men of the PRUs fly either in Spitfires or Mosquitoes, the latter for the very long-range jobs. The aircraft have holes cut in the fuselage to accommodate precision cameras for taking oblique or vertical photographs. Whenever the result of a latest raid is needed, a PRU aircraft braves weather and Axis defences to obtain a vital photograph.

The range of the Units based in Britain extends from the north of Norway to Gibraltar, and improvements in technique, equipment and camera installation have overcome the difficulties as navigation of a single-seat machine in which the pilot must do the work of a whole crew, of freezing cameras and of condensation on lenses, as well as the necessity to fly at greater heights to evade defences. Most photographic reconnaissance is carried out from a high altitude, but it also includes very low-level work, known to the pilots as 'dicing' (from the cliche 'dicing with death'). It is highly dangerous work, but has produced excellent results. The most spectacular photographs obtained by the British-based PRUs were those of the German dams before and after they had been breached.

An idea of the demand for aerial photographs can be seen from the fact that between April and June 1940, when the unit was in its infancy, 127,350 contact prints were made with 32,340 enlargements and 780 plots. In a single day in October 1941, 9,786 photographs were taken. Today the work has been so greatly extended that in a busy week some hundreds of gallons of hypo are used in processing the pictures and machines are used which can produce 1,000 prints an hour.

IN THE NEWS

Friday 10   **"Call Up Deferments to End"** In view of the urgent need for men in the forces, the Government has decided that deferments granted for qualifying men in munitions and other industries must end.

Saturday 11   **"Unique Cinematic Record"** A British surgeon has been filmed performing an operation for cancer of the lung. The film is made for demonstrating to doctors all over the world, an operation which was carried out for the first time only ten years ago.

Sunday 12   **"Plimsolls for the Children"** To ease the child shoe shortage, plimsolls are now being manufactured throughout the country. They are made of rubber or synthetic rubber.

Monday 13   **"King's Trees Felled"** Owing to elm disease, trees on the south of the Long Walk at Windsor, planted by Charles II in 1684 are being felled. Replanting will be with plane and horse chestnuts.

Tuesday 14   **"First Woman MP in Australia"** Dame Enid Lyons, widow of the late Prime Minister of Australia, has won Darwin, Tasmania, for the United Australia Party in the recent election and become the first woman to enter the House of Representatives.

Wednesday 15 **"Food Facts and Fallacies"** A major food scientist has debunked the fallacy that dehydration affects food values. Fresh eggs have the same nutrients as dried eggs and dried milk, reconstituted with water, is practically equal to fresh milk.

Thursday 16   **"Rural Workers Cottages"** The Minister of Health officially opened two cottages built by Tonbridge Rural Council, the first completed under the emergency rural housing scheme. They were completed in 11 weeks, a creditable enough achievement in peace-time, and remarkable under war-time conditions.

HERE IN BRITAIN
"Pet Plans"

The government issued a pamphlet about how to care for pets during wartime. Along with advice on first aid and how to evacuate their animals from cities, they also suggested that owners consider having their pets "painlessly destroyed." Fearing possible food shortages and roving packs of starved dogs, thousands complied. In the span of only one week, as many as 750,000 pets were euthanised by their owners or by animal shelters. The London Zoo, meanwhile, had all of its poisonous animals killed to prevent them from escaping in the event of a bomb attack.

AROUND THE WORLD
"Black Market Readers"

In Japan, the black market in American newspapers and magazines has now reached an incredible point at which up to £15 is being paid for a single issue of certain newspapers from New York. This is because the American Daily Press is not on sale in this country, while the ever-increasing eagerness of a band of journalists and agents of a certain belligerent country, to get copies, has sent the prices rocketing. These men's touts approach Clippers on their arrival in the country with ridiculous offers for any paper that they may be carrying.

BLOOD FOR THE ARMY

He gave *his* blood..
Will you give yours?

Blood for the Armed Forces

The blood of up to 20 donors may be needed for one casualty, therefore it is imperative to maintain a highly efficient service, and this is provided by the Army Blood Transfusion Service, who have 320,000 registered, voluntary donors in the south of England. Of these, some 3,000 to 4,000 have been bled each week for many months but the need for donors is constant and increasing so six major campaigns are run a year and minor campaigns run continuously. Bleeding is carried out by mobile teams who are quartered in towns from where they cover the surrounding areas. Miniature hospital wards are set up in 20 minutes in a works canteen or village schoolroom, the blood is taken painlessly and simply and after a rest of about 20 minutes most donors return to work.

The blood groups AB, A, and B can only be given to cases in their own grouping, but the fourth group, 0, is universal. This is pooled and most of it separated, clarified, and filtered to make fluid plasma for use by military units at home and in temperate climates. For tropical and sub-tropical areas, the plasma is dried and sent to units complete with distilled water for reconstitution. In 1941 the service was presented with its own plasma drying plant by the 'Silver Thimble Fund of the Women of India'. It carries out a highly technical operation known as the spin-freezing process. Twelve to fourteen hundred bottles a week can be dried by this plant and 105,973 pints have been sent out. Whole blood is exported to any theatre of war within air distance from England and blood banks are maintained in important civil and RAF centres. Whole blood which remains unused after three to four weeks is then converted into plasma.

SEPT 17TH - 23RD 1943

IN THE NEWS

Friday 17   **"Miners Returning to Work"** Fifteen thousand miners who have been on strike in Nottinghamshire over the imprisonment of a 15-year-old surface worker who refused to work underground, have returned to work.

Saturday 18   **"American Gifts to Britain"** One gift the 'British War Relief Society of America' is to present this year, is £30,000 to the Queen Victoria Cottage Hospital at East Grinstead which specialises in facial plastic surgery.

Sunday 19   **"Mr Churchill's Arduous Tour"** The Prime Minister arrived back in London to a great welcome at Euston after a long visit to Canada and the US. He repaid the waiting crowds with his customary V sign.

Monday 20   **"Design for Speedy Vessels"** In a shipyard on the north-east coast is the first of a series of large and fast cargo ships of standard design. They are the answer to the demand for bigger ships capable of maintaining a speed of at least 15 knots.

Tuesday 21   **"Archbishop in Moscow"** The Archbishop of York attended a special service in Moscow Cathedral. He said, *"I have flown nearly 7,000 miles to tell the holy Orthodox Church of Russia and the people of this great nation of the great sympathy of the Church of England with you all in your terrible sufferings".*

Wednesday 22   **"Counsellor of State"** The King recommended the revision of the Regency Act and, although she is still a minor, Princess Elizabeth is to be appointed a Counsellor of State in the event of his absence from the country.

Thursday 23   **"Women's Wits Wanted"** Issued by the Ministry of Information: 'Industry and Government departments are in urgent need of intelligent women for engineering draughtsmanship, production planning, radio research and scientific instrument design'.

HERE IN BRITAIN

"Fifty Million Books"

The target set last October of 50 million books in the national book recovery and salvage campaign has been reached in only 11 months. It is estimated that 5,000 book scrutineers examined the 50 million volumes collected and sorted them into three categories.

Those for the services (7m), those for restocking war-damaged libraries (1.5m) and the 41.5m which had no value were suitable for repulping to make munitions.

AROUND THE WORLD

"American Red Cross"

The American Red Cross runs a 'Club on Wheels'. These are converted buses and carry American newspapers and magazines, writing materials, American doughnuts, coffee, cigarettes and chewing gum to men on duty in isolated camps and air bases. Each one is staffed by three American girls and the latest gramophone records are performed from loudspeakers on the roof. The 'clubmobiles' have served 2 million doughnuts and 12 million cups of coffee and can be converted into a 10-stretcher ambulance.

To be able to distinguish between friendly and hostile aircraft without mistake or delay is obviously of vital importance to every anti-aircraft gunner. To recognise any type of aircraft flying in that theatre of war is a stiff test, but ingenious and sometimes unorthodox training methods are used in the training schools. The courses are arranged to make the subject a fascinating hobby, rather than a tedious task to be learnt and are compressed into a fortnight.

A sergeant instructor explains how to find distinctive features. For instance, the fuselage of an FW190 is shaped like a carrot or a cribbage-board peg; a Heinkel 111 is easy to identify by the pieces 'bitten out' of the trailing edge of the wing near the roots, and so on. In a small cinema 10 silhouettes are flashed on the screen for only one second each and the students write down each type. Another room houses a large model aircraft, the components of which are all detachable and the students learn the technical terms and elements of aircraft construction.

An ingenious device known as a 'miniature range' enables students to study model aircraft under conditions approximating to the real thing. A model, which can be turned in any direction, is suspended in front of an artificial sky, and as the student watches it in a mirror, the aircraft can be made to appear to approach or recede by altering the distance of the mirror. Lighting conditions can also be altered to represent full daylight or dusk. An amusing, but effective, way of keeping the student interested is by means of specially adapted games. There are aircraft jigsaw puzzles, a variation of the popular old game of 'housey housey,' with aircraft instead of numbers and dice with aircraft features inscribed on each side instead of dots.

SEPT 24TH - 30TH 1943

IN THE NEWS

Friday 24   **"Brighter Torches"** You no longer need to dim torches with a piece of newspaper, though the light shown is still limited to a circle one inch in diameter because, to economise with batteries, flash lamp bulbs will in future be of a lower amperage.

Saturday 25   **"'Bacon Sympathising' Vandals"** Shakespeare memorials in Stratford on Avon were daubed with red paint; facial features painted on the four dials of the American memorial fountain clock and a piece of ladies' underwear was left flying from the flagstaff of the town hall.

Sunday 26   **"Battle of Britain Sunday"** The day was commemorated nation-wide with services of thanksgiving and processions. The King and Queen led their people in an act of remembrance at a morning service at St. Paul's Cathedral.

Monday 27   **"Now Scottish Miners Strike"** Seven Lanarkshire pits employing nearly 3,000 miners were idle protesting against the arrest of six miners who failed to pay fines of £5 each, imposed in connection with a previous unofficial strike.

Tuesday 28   **"50,000 Boys Wanted"** A nationwide recruiting campaign for bright lads to join the Air Training Corps has been opened to maintain the strength of the corps. Every week, hundreds of cadets are leaving for service in the RAF, Fleet Air Arm or Army.

Wednesday 29   **"Government's First Conference of Women"** Six thousand women from every part of Great Britain attended the Albert Hall and heard the Prime Minister's praises for their essential part in the war effort.

Thursday 30   **"Lack of Veterinary Professionals"** Experts have called for better education for veterinary professionals. Fewer than 3,000 veterinary surgeons are active in Britain.

HERE IN BRITAIN
"Queen Mary's Needlework Guild"

The London Guild has packed over 19,000 garments for distribution to needy cases through charities and missions. Queen Mary herself knitted 12 woollen cot covers and collected 3,300 garments including women's woollen underwear from the Queen and men's underwear from the King. The Princess Royal has collected 350 garments and knitted 12 men's pullovers. The recipients pay nothing for the clothes but must give up coupons. To become an associate member of the Guild it is necessary to give two garments in one year.

AROUND THE WORLD
"Pyrethrum Seed from Kenya"

Kenya has become the world's principal source of supply of pyrethrum seed and 20,000 lb is now being collected for delivery to Russia to replant 7,500 acres of war devastated Caucasian fields. Recently, 10,000 lb was sent to Brazil, 5,000 lb to India and smaller quantities to Egypt, Australia, Nyasaland, Nigeria, Ceylon, Jamaica and the Belgian Congo. The country thus provides one of the most important allied war supplies, among the uses of which are a protection for troops against malaria in tropical countries and a preservative of stored foods.

MUSIC FOR THE FORCES

A festival of daily concerts was held this week at a large RAF centre in Wales and was the second of its kind and not likely to be the last. The Entertainments National Service Association (ENSA) established in 1939 to provide entertainment for British armed forces personnel has obligations to provide serious music as well as light-hearted frivolity for its clients and it takes these obligations seriously. In fact, it might be more careful about the quality of this fare provided. This RAF concert was staged in co-operation with the BBC who has at its disposal a first-class orchestra and conductors.

Both ENSA and the BBC have staffs to deal with the transport, billeting, advertising and the thousand and one details necessary to ensure that the eminent solo artists, whose services they can both command, shall be on the platform of the hall and not on that of a remote railway station when the concert is due to begin! The BBC can also, at the same time, carry out its obligations to provide symphony music for the public by broadcasting these concerts.

ENSA, besides organising large festivals such as were enjoyed by the Army at Aldershot and the Navy at Portsmouth before the RAF festival of last week, regularly supplies gramophone records and small, miscellaneous concert programmes, while the education officers keep an eye on the weekly gramophone recitals and get lecturers to come in occasionally and talk about music. At the RAF station where this latest festival was held, two evening classes a week were devoted to 'theoretical and practical music' and on Tuesdays there was always a gramophone recital. Some men have discovered music since they joined the Army, and the listening groups give the impression to the visiting lecturers that they have found in music an 'interest for life'.

Oct 1st - 7th 1943

IN THE NEWS

Friday Oct 1   **"£25 Million Raised"** In the first four years of the war, the many Red Cross and St John War Organisations have benefited greatly since repatriated prisoners of war have told of lives being saved by Red Cross parcels.

Saturday 2   **"Lanarkshire Miners Back"** 3,000 men still on strike are expected back to work after the release of 16 miners who were imprisoned for refusing to pay the fines for taking part in a previous unofficial stoppage.

Sunday 3   **"Boy's Brigade Diamond Jubilee"** In the beginning, 30 boys met in a Glasgow mission hall. The Brigade now has 132,000 members in the British Isles and many thousands more in the Dominions and Colonies.

Monday 4   **"Chaplin's Girl Has Daughter"** Before Joan Barry's baby was twelve hours old, she was the centre of a legal case. Footprints were taken for court records and Chaplin, who denies he is the father, is paying the medical expenses pending paternity blood tests.

Tuesday 5   **"Tribute to the Sea Cadet Corps"** The First Lord of the Admiralty opened a Navy League exhibition in London and emphasised the importance of the Corps in recruiting for the Royal Navy and the Merchant Navy.

Wednesday 6   **"Shoddy Shoes for Children"** 30 million pairs are made a year and the Board of Trade has labelled many examples as 'disgraceful'. All footwear is to carry the registered number of the manufacturer to enable tracing of the makers of boots and shoes of poor quality.

Thursday 7   **"Prisoners' Toys"** Toys are being made from wood salvaged from blitzed buildings, by inmates in 15 prisons. They provide rocking horses, railway engines, wheelbarrows, blackboards and easels urgently needed by the Nursery School Association.

HERE IN BRITAIN
"Fox Cubs on the Prom"

For the first time in living memory, foxes are breeding on Brighton front. Recently people have seen, in the early morning and evening, a fine dog fox with his vixen and a litter of five cubs playing round the bandstand on the eastern promenade. They have an earth beneath the bandstand, and the family find plenty of shelter and food. On the outskirts of the town foxes have become such a menace that smallholders and farmers have had to organise shooting parties to keep them down and hen roosts well inside the borough limit have been raided night after night.

AROUND THE WORLD
"Milk Famine in New York"

New Yorkers are facing a milk crisis and already 500,000 families have been deprived of their usual supplies whilst supplies to hospitals and other institutions and the armed forces stationed there are threatened. The crisis was caused by a mass walk out by several thousand employees of the two largest distributing companies. They are protesting against the decision by the War Labour Board to permit the firms to lay off 1,000 of their delivery men. Previously the Office of Defence Transportation had ordered the companies to stop making daily deliveries and deliver on alternate days.

BRITISH WOODLANDS

Women played a vital role in managing and working the forests, from planting to thinning to felling and preparing the felled timber.

The importance of forestry as a branch of rural economy is beginning to receive a greater appreciation than in the past. After the devastation of the last war, the Forestry Commission was set up in 1919, with power to acquire land for afforestation and private forestry was also encouraged by contributions towards the cost of planting. The Government is to pursue a vigorous forestry policy after this war and asks that the nation devotes 5,000,000 acres - approximately one-eleventh of the total land area - to forest over the next 50 years to ensure national safety and reasonable insurance against future shortages in world supplies. It would also benefit the development and settlement of rural Britain.

The forest unit at Rendlesham in Suffolk may be regarded as an epitome of the larger work of the Commission. Much of the land now growing trees was producing nothing but weeds and rabbits before. Conifers do best under such conditions and Scots pine and Corsican pine are the main species cultivated and over 6,000 acres have been planted here. Operations begin with the planting of 2,000 trees to the acre and they reach maturity after 60 or 70 years. Close planting is practised to ensure straightness of stem and the trees are gradually thinned out to help the growth of the most vigorous trees whilst the less vigorous trees are felled for pit wood and other war purposes. Mobile saw benches are used in the open and women who had not been accustomed to manual labour before the war, are proving expert sawyers. Rendlesham Forest employs 60 men, 30 women and 25 juveniles and new industries which will absorb a very large part of the produce of the forest are expected to spring up and lead to the creation of new village communities with a prosperous and permanently employed population.

OCT 8TH-14TH 1943

IN THE NEWS

Friday 8   **"Bandits in Belfast"** A policeman was shot dead after escorting the weekly payroll from a bank, another example of the terrorism by bandits in the city where people are afraid to come forward and give evidence.

Saturday 9   **"The Pope 'Virtually a Prisoner'"** A statement in Liverpool states, 'In the latest outrage against religion, his Holiness Pope Pius XII is virtually a prisoner at the hands of the Germans without freedom of access to his spiritual children throughout the world'.

Sunday 10   **"Safest Roads of the War"** The fourth year of the war has the lowest total of deaths from road accidents up to the end of August. Whilst improvement may be due to the smaller volume of traffic, drivers, cyclists and pedestrians are generally taking more precautions.

Monday 11   **"Answer to Vandals"** The management of the Shakespeare Memorial Theatre believe servicemen were responsible for the recent 'red paint' vandalism in Stratford on Avon and have withdrawn their cheap tickets until it is cleaned up.

Tuesday 12   **"New Leather Will Not 'Melt'"** The shoddy-leather problem for children's boots and shoes has been blamed on imported South American ready-tanned leather. Whilst suitable for hot countries, it cannot stand up to the wet, changeable British climate.

Wednesday 13 **"Oranges"** Eighty-four million oranges have arrived in the country from South Africa and every child up to the age of 16 will have a share.

Thursday 14   **"No Nationalisation of Mines"** Mr Churchill assured the House of Commons he would bar the takeover of the coal industry without a general election.

HERE IN BRITAIN
"Communal Restaurants"

There are now more than 2,000 of these war-time restaurants throughout the country and they answer the needs of the adult population of all ages and both sexes. Both professional and manual workers use them and about 8% of the diners are the elderly, who get a full meal at a special price.

Before, many of the restaurant's customers ate their meals at home, but a large proportion of them were women who now go out to work. About 27% of the diners used to take sandwiches to work and 40% ate in commercial restaurants or cafes. They have become regular customers.

AROUND THE WORLD
"Little Ship's Long Voyage"

A captain in the Merchant Navy, took an egg-shaped, 300-ton crane-ship, 15,200 miles, including a passage round the Cape, to Turkey. The voyage was an extraordinary feat of navigation, as the ship, called 'Turkish Delight' by the crew, was built exclusively for use in sheltered waters and is only 10ft long.

She was so difficult to steer that for months it was thought that she would never be able to leave the Clyde. Yet for 10 months she was taken, unescorted, through gales, heavy seas, and waters in which enemy U-boats were operating and was delivered safely.

ROYAL OBSERVER CORPS

The Royal Observer Corps is nearly 30 years old, is some 40,000 strong, and has been doing a vital front-line job every second of the day and night since a week before the outbreak of the present war. Briefly, their main task is to spot and plot the course of every aircraft, both hostile and friendly, which is over or approaching these shores. Throughout Britain there are 1,500 carefully sited observer posts, each manned every minute of the 24 hours by two highly trained observers. They are liable to have any one of nearly 300 types of friendly and hostile aircraft over their posts which are often situated in outlandish spots, on a hill or a headland, on top of a church tower or even on top of a tree in a pine wood.

They are manned day and night in every type of weather, and the spotters 'tell' every outgoing or incoming aircraft by direct telephone line to the nearest ROC centre, of which there are 40 conveniently scattered about the country. Here there is a table like those in use in Fighter operations rooms, on which the course of the aircraft is plotted. The centre in its turn keeps Fighter Command abreast of the situation and is an ever-present means for the RAF to keep a constant check on any developments. It is on information from the men and women of ROC that air raid warnings are sounded.

For security reasons the public have heard little of the ROC, they have not heard, for instance, of the countless lives which have been saved by ROC information on 'homing' crippled bombers returning from the Continent, nor of the many lives saved by alerting Air-Sea rescue to aircraft down in the sea.

IN THE NEWS

Friday 15   **"Steel Lifeboats"** An initial order has been made by the Ministry for a new design of steel lifeboats for oil tankers. The boat has a sliding asbestos canopy to provide protection from oil fire at sea.

Saturday 16   **"ATS 5th Birthday"** More than 2,000 women of the ATS marched past the Queen, their Commandant-in-Chief, in front of Buckingham Palace and afterwards attended a service at Westminster Abbey.

Sunday 17   **"Switch for Winter Production"** Munitions production has been switched from basic items such as guns and ammunition to an emphasis on invasion craft, bridging materials, cranes, and needs for rapid movement of armies by land, sea or air.

Monday 18   **"Coming of Age"** The Borough of Watford has come of age but celebrations have not been possible. Watford figured in the Peasant Rising of 1381, was not untouched by the Great Plague of 1665 and has possessed a public market since Henry I's time.

Tuesday 19   **"Human Guinea Pigs"** There are plans to test 100 children with painless experiments using certain drugs of the sulphonamide group. Doctors hope for a tremendous reduction in the number of British children crippled by rheumatism and other cardiac troubles.

Wednesday 20 **"East Meets West"** A community centre for men, women and children of all races is being established in Liverpool centre. It is an attempt to break down colour prejudice and furnish the community with a non-political and non-sectarian focus for their social life.

Thursday 21   **"Emigration to Australia"** The Australian Government is examining the prospects of assisted immigration on a large scale from the UK after the war. They believe there is ample scope for the employment of workers from British industry.

HERE IN BRITAIN
"Wakey Wakey"

For nearly three years the sound of an alarm clock has not been heard in Leeds and timekeeping has not been the same since the 'knockers up' joined up. When, four months ago, there was mention of 60,000 American alarm clocks arriving, essential workers clapped each other on the back - and when the clocks failed to materialise, they took it with Yorkshire stoicism. Recently another few thousand clocks were expected and 4,000 workers applied for permits. It was computed that Leeds should get at least six of them, but never a clock, never a permit, has made an appearance.

AROUND THE WORLD
"Repatriation of Wounded"

The return of British Empire and United States disabled prisoners of war from Germany under the provisions of the Geneva Convention is in progress, and the first parties are being embarked at Gothenburg for the voyage home. A British hospital ship and transport delivered German prisoners of war from camps in the United Kingdom, Canada and the United States to Gothenburg. For the return voyage they will be joined by a Swedish ship, and the three ships will bring back to the UK more than 4,000 men, all of whom have been brought by train, from German prisoner of war camps.

TRAFALGAR DAY

Sunday 21st October
Trafalgar Day Lunch

Join us to commemorate
Nelson's famous victory

The Trafalgar Day celebration at the foot of Nelson's Column in Trafalgar Square on Thursday included the reading of a new short poem, 'Men of the Royal Navy,' written for the occasion by the Poet Laureate, Mr. John Masefield. A large crowd gathered to watch and listen. Three admirals attended the ceremony and a band of the Royal Marines played on the north side of Trafalgar Square where, on the pavement below was drawn up a guard of honour of the Sea Cadet Corps. Royal Marine buglers sounded a fanfare and a Sea Cadet bugler, standing on the plinth of Nelson's Column, sounded 'Attention' before words praising Nelson, the beloved admiral, and his comrades, were spoken. The Royal Marine buglers sounded Last Post and official wreaths were placed at the base of the Column. After after one minute's silence, Reveille was played and then came Nelson's 'Noble Prayer Before Trafalgar'. Finally, a verse of 'Eternal Father, strong to save' was sung and the National Anthem concluded the affair.

Trafalgar Day is an annual celebration observed on October 21. It commemorates the victory of the Royal Navy against the French and Spanish naval forces at the Battle of Trafalgar in 1805. In 1805, France was the dominant military force led by Napoleon, a great soldier. However, the Royal Navy ruled the seas. On the Franco-Spanish front were 33-line ships, five frigates and two brigs, while the Royal Navy had 27-line ships, four frigates, one schooner and one cutter. Nelson captured 18 French ships, forcing Admiral Villeneuve to surrender. The British fleet he commanded consisted of warships built of wood, driven by sails, and equipped on both sides with cannons. The Battle of Trafalgar was significant, confirming the superiority of the British Royal Navy but also marking the death of Admiral Horatio Nelson aboard HMS Victory.

OCT 22ND-28TH 1943

IN THE NEWS

Friday 22   **"Aircraft Carriers of 45,000 Tons"** The US Navy is building three which will be the largest ships of their kind in the world, capable of carrying big 2 engine bombers and better protected than any other carriers.

Saturday 23   **"Greatest Harvest in History"** More land has been given up for aerodromes, battle training grounds and such like, so we have grown a record amount of food from the smallest acreage devoted since records began.

Sunday 24   **"Inquiry into Work Hindered at Docks"** Obsolete practices have come down from a different era of surplus and casual employment but today, when labour is scarce, they stand in the way of the rapid unloading of vital cargoes.

Monday 25   **"Hot Water and No Smoke"** An electrical town heating system estimated to cost £1,500,000 has been put before Bristol City Council. All homes would be able to turn on the heat at the flick of a switch and eliminate hundreds of smoke-emitting chimneys.

Tuesday 26   **"Solving the Problems of Marriage"** The Marriage Guidance Council, which was resumed a year ago, is to begin an educational campaign emphasising the vital importance of the family unit as the basis of community life.

Wednesday 27 **"The USS Lafayette Ready for Refitting"** The salving of the former French liner ' Normandie', which caught fire in New York Harbour in February last year, has been completed and she is to be refitted as a transport vessel.

Thursday 28   **"Czechoslovakia's Silver Jubilee"** There will be no public observance in London as it is recognised that the proper place for celebrations is Prague where the day will stir many memories of the price people have paid for their determination to be free.

HERE IN BRITAIN

"Home Guard – Battle of London"

All Home Guard and Civil Defence units took part in the biggest scale exercise ever held in London. They were called out in the early morning to deal with 'airborne invaders' who attacked more than 100 scattered points. Thunder flashes and blank cartridges resounded in the quiet streets and the 'battle' was fought with great vigour.

At vital factories the attackers were dealt with easily by the factory Home Guard but one party of the 'enemy' captured motorboats on the Thames and made a water-borne landing with success.

AROUND THE WORLD

"Chows to Washington"

"It is the concern entirely of the Ministry of Home Security," an official said at the outcry and 'dogs protest' at being rejected by the Army. Collies and Chows have been declared ineligible for the canine division of the American Army, much to the anger of their fans. The official reason for rejecting collies is that *'they've had the brains bred out of them'* while Chows are despised *"because they have been found to be unreliable."* The Collie Club of America has protested and a delegation of Chows – of proven reliability – may go to Washington.

PoWs Welcomed Home

The 'Empress of Russia' and the 'Drottningholm' arrived off Leith this week carrying 3,500 repatriated prisoners of war. Awaiting their arrival was a message of cordial greetings from the King and Queen. Overnight the large reception shed had been decorated with flags of the United Nations and a large banner bearing the word 'Welcome' was hung above the gangway. Inside the main shed mobile canteens served tea, coffee and hot milk, and voluntary workers had prepared over 7,000 sandwiches. Red Cross workers distributed slabs of chocolate, apples, cigarettes and matches. Dock workers, voluntary workers and nurses gave the men a rousing cheer as they came ashore, and the men made a spirited reply. The pipers and military band of The King's Own Scottish Borderers struck up 'Roll out the barrel' and the men responded with a rousing chorus.

Most of the men were in complete battledress and a few had makeshift hats, like three Royal Scots who had knitted themselves Balmorals from old socks and torn pullovers, but they all had one thing in common, brightly polished boots. A surprising number carried musical instruments, and one of the first off was carrying a double bass, which had brightened lonely spells in the prison camp. Some carried attaché cases, others had kit bags and packs which they had skilfully manufactured out of odd materials in the camps. One man had an excellent metal representation of his regimental badge. He had melted down silver papers from cigarette packets and so fashioned the badge, in a mould. The incident was typical of the ingenuity displayed by the men in confinement. Among the comforts waiting for the men were bundles of newspapers, which they eagerly scanned for news of the progress of the war. *"We've a lot of reading to make up,"* said one.

OCT 29TH - NOV 4TH 1943

IN THE NEWS

Friday 29 — **"Aid to Russia Fund"** Mrs Churchill's fund has passed £4,000,000. She said, *"This sum of money is small compared with the size of Russia, the number of her wrecked cities and of her heroic, unconquerable population, but it is a token from the hearts of all British people all over the world."*

Saturday 30 — **"Agreement in Moscow"** President Roosevelt has confirmed that the Moscow tripartite conference has been 'a tremendous success' culminating in the issuing of the Moscow Declaration.

Sunday 31 — **"Medical Service for Civil Servants"** The Post Office has had a medical service since 1855, the largest industrial medical service in the country, and now all Government departments are to have one too.

Monday Nov 1 — **"Slag Heaps on Football Pitches"** The war time increase in coal production in South Wales has meant slag heaps are growing and spreading too quickly and threatening to overwhelm some treasured communal Rugby football pitches.

Tuesday 2 — **"Make Do and Mend"** There has been a make-do-and-mend exhibition in Harrods. People have been responding well but a recent judgement that the savings of a wife from her housekeeping is not hers to keep, but her husband's, has dulled interest.

Wednesday 3 — **"Strike for Equal Pay"** 24,000 workers, mainly women, are idle in a group of West of Scotland factories. Women want equal pay for equal machining work.

Thursday 4 — **"Christmas Food Supplies"** Arrangements for ensuring an equitable distribution of a 'fairly substantial' supply of Christmas turkeys and poultry, and the arrival here of Canadian apples for the first time for two years, were announced by the Minister of Food.

HERE IN BRITAIN
"Old Sheffield Plate"

Sheffield has acquired a collection of old Sheffield plate, comprising over 600 pieces and was collected over many years by an old family firm, Bradbury's, who have made old Sheffield plate since the 18th century.

Plate came into existence with the discovery by Thomas Bolsover that silver and copper readily fused. This led to manufacturers making simple articles such as buttons and snuffboxes of copper with a veneer of silver. Gradually the industry included the whole range of articles usually made in solid silver.

AROUND THE WORLD
"Long Distance Sheep"

150 New Zealand sheep have just finished a journey of more than 7,000 miles which took over a year. It started in 1941, when China ordered the sheep.

They were at sea when Japan entered the war and Hong Kong and Rangoon fell, so they were diverted to India and then the Himalayas. Making their way over the mountains they were held up for some lambs to be born. Now the original 150 plus the lambs have finally made it to their new Chinese home.

SPIRIDONOVKA PALACE

The Third Moscow Conference between the major Allies, where the Moscow Declaration was issued, took place at the Kremlin but the delegates also met at the Spiridonovka Palace in Moscow. This Palace was built by an eccentric called Arseny Morozon, the younger son of a Moscow textile 'king'. Born into great wealth, he was uninterested in his father's business, leaving that to an equally eccentric, prolific art collecting, older brother, and young Arseny engaged in a hedonistic life, indulging his greatest passions, hunting and dog-breeding. In the late 1890's he was consumed with an additional passion, building a Gothic-Moorish castle next to his mother's classical mansion on Volkhonka Street, on a plot she offered him on his 25th birthday. Inspired by the faux-medieval Pena Palace in Portugal, Arseny reproduced that mishmash of styles, adding a facade copied from the House of Shells in Salamanca. The building provoked widespread ridicule even before it was completed, being absurdly out of place in central Moscow. Tolstoy, in his book 'The Resurrection' has a passer-by describe the building as a *'stupid unnecessary palace for a stupid useless person'.*

If the exterior was eccentric, the interior decoration followed suit, reflecting an absolute eclecticism of styles. From pseudo-Gothic to Empire, from Arabic to Chinese, the Palace is filled with carved woodwork, Persian carpets, brocade hangings, marble mantelpieces, white and gold, satin upholstered, Empire furniture and stained glass. After the Revolution, the Palace became the theatre, 'Proletkult' until 1928, then the embassy of different countries and even the editions of British newspapers and is now the Reception House for the Soviet Foreign Minister. In the Music Room, where the meetings probably took place, hangs a painting presented by the British Government of Anthony Eden signing, in the presence of Churchill, Molotov and Maisky, the Anglo Soviet Treaty of May last year.

Nov 5TH - 11TH 1943

IN THE NEWS

Friday 5 **"Merchant Navy Extra Comforts"** Of 15 special coupons, 8 will be marked J for the jerseys the 250,000 women volunteer knitters have ceaselessly supplied over four years, 2 marked M for muffler, 4 marked S for socks and one marked G for gloves.

Saturday 6 **"Domestics: Volunteer or Be Called Up"** Unless 10,000 volunteers are forthcoming immediately, women are to be called up for domestic service in hospitals and other public institutions.

Sunday 7 **"Anniversary of the Soviet Union"** The twenty-fifth anniversary was celebrated in London at the Stoll Theatre. The Dean of Canterbury resided and said, *"we are present to congratulate Russia on what she has done. After the enemy has been vanquished, we should together enter on the task of building up a new world."*

Monday 8 **"Homes for Honeymooners"** Of 25,000 houses to be built by Leeds City Council, 3,000 are reserved for newly-weds so they can have a better start to their married lives.

Tuesday 9 **"Golden Arrow"** The Royal Signals have a new, mobile, high-speed wireless station for keeping armies in the field in touch with GHQ . It is named after the famous London-Paris boat-train because troops and equipment is carried in long train-like motor-vehicles.

Wednesday 10 **"Housekeeping Savings"** The Lord Chancellor is to receive a deputation from angry women, asking for amendments to the Married Women's Property Act to allow a working housewife the right to an equal share of the family income.

Thursday 11 **"New 'Vim' Drink for Young Workers"** Industrial war workers up to age 18 are to have a 'pleasant' drink called Milcoco. Its basic contents are processed milk, sugar and cocoa and will be sold at 1d a cup.

HERE IN BRITAIN
"Seaweed Products"

Most of us have a vague idea that iodine is extracted from seaweed and have, half seriously used seaweed as a barometer. This week, some of the by-products of seaweed were described by a lecturer in Botany at Liverpool University. Extremely good custard powder, a 'white satin wedding gown', curtain material like artificial silk, sheets of paper as transparent as glass and as tough as steel. For two years the scientist has been working on seaweed research taking a group of students to an island where they turned 'mermaid' and dived to fix labels to seaweed to measure the rate of growth.

AROUND THE WORLD
"Foiling the Smugglers"

The Royal Navy is foiling a German smuggling racket in neutral ships which, unknown to captains or owners, often carry precious war cargoes across the Atlantic. These include industrial diamonds, platinum, mica, food extracts and much more, hidden in other cargo. The Germans started their new racket after the Brazilian Government closed down the 'Italian Lati' airline used by them to carry small articles with the highest value to their war effort. To stop this traffic, the Navy is making fuller use of its belligerent rights of 'visit and search'.

POPPY DAY

It is a quarter of a century ago since the Armistice of 11 November 1918, brought the fighting in the first world war to a close. On this fifth war-time observance of the anniversary, the King decided in the present circumstances, the usual service at the Cenotaph would not be held. Poppy Day was however observed, forty million poppies, made by disabled ex-service men in the British Legion Poppy Factory at Richmond, were sold in aid of Lord Haig's Fund and a Day of Remembrance service was held on November 7th.

Civic heads laid wreaths at town war memorials, and other wreaths were placed on the memorials at factories, offices, and institutions of various kinds. In London wreaths were laid at the Cenotaph, on the tomb of the Unknown Warrior in Westminster Abbey, and at the Mercantile Marine War Memorial on Tower Hill. Whilst the 11 strokes from Big Ben were heard above the traffic around the Cenotaph and outside Westminster, the signal for 'Two Minutes Silence' was not given in view of the risk of confusion with the air raid warning signals.

The President of the British Legion wrote: For more than 20 years, Poppy Day has financed the British Legion, the country's greatest benevolent organisation for ex-service men. It has brought comfort and hope into hundreds of thousands of ex-service homes. But in the future, it must do more than ever before. There is now another generation of ex-servicemen, and women too, needing a helping hand. Over a hundred thousand of this new generation have been helped already, thanks to Poppy Day. The legion's work is growing steadily, month by month and it will reach its peak after the war has ended, and we must not fail our fighting men when their service is done, and their need is greatest.

Nov 12TH-18TH 1943

IN THE NEWS

Friday 12   **"Lord Woolton Moving On"** Lord Woolton, Minister of Food, has been appointed to plan the 'new' Britain as Minister of Reconstruction.

Saturday 13   **"Winter Transport for War Workers"** The Ministry of Labour has granted exceptional priority to getting people to the factories this winter. Overriding preference will be given to the filling of vacancies for omnibus conductresses.

Sunday 14   **"The BBC Celebrates"** The BBC celebrated its twenty-first anniversary today and received congratulations from the King. A feature programme, 'Twenty-One Today' gave a picture of events covering the four phases in its history

Monday 15   **"A Pink Pill Cure"** A pill to cure and prevent seasickness has been developed by the Royal Canadian Navy. The formula is a war secret, but the capsules will soon be issued to ships. Taken one or two hours before sailing or in rough weather, they can remain effective for eight hours.

Tuesday 16   **"The RAF Needs You"** About 50 trades and service callings in the RAF are now open for volunteers generally up to the age of 55 and probably for a limited period only. Men are needed as carpenters, fitters, mechanics, instrument repairers and even meteorologists.

Wednesday 17 **"Turkeys for Christmas"** The Ministry estimates there will be 1.6 million turkeys available to be sold on controlled prices. Half have been reared in Britain, 500,000 from Eire and 300,000 from Northern Ireland.

Thursday 18   **"Uproar at Mosley's Release"** The Home Secretary has announced that Sir Oswald Mosley, the man who introduced Fascism to Britain, is to be released from Holloway prison where he has been held since 1940, on medical grounds.

HERE IN BRITAIN

"Civilians Leave the South-West"

3,000 people must leave their homes before the end of December to make room for a battle training ground for the United States Army. Some of the inhabitants did not yet know where they were going or when they will be able to return to their homes and farms. The area includes 200 farms and must be completely cleared. An American general told one gathering *"The hardship you are suffering will be compensated by the lives of Americans and Britishers that will be saved by what the men learn during their training in this area."*

AROUND THE WORLD

"Goodbye Bully"

The Australian Army catering service has been working on an improved substitute for 'bully and biscuit'. The new ration is contained in an air-tight tin eight by four by two inches which when opened can be used as a billy. Inside are three packages each weighing 1lb, representing one complete meal and sealed in waterproof paper. Two packages a day adequately maintain one soldier in the field. Each package also contains four tea tablets, two sugar tablets, two salt tablets and skim milk powder. Gaps in the packages are filled with barley sugar.

FEEDING WARTIME BRITAIN

WASTE NOT—WANT NOT

PREPARE FOR WINTER

Save Perishable Foods by Preserving <u>Now</u>

LORD WOOLTON PIE

THE OFFICIAL RECIPE

In hotels and restaurants, no less than in communal canteens, many people have tasted Lord Woolton pie and pronounced it good. Like many another economical dish, it can be described as wholesome fare. It also meets the dietician's requirements in certain vitamins. The ingredients can be varied according to the vegetables in season. Here is the official recipe:—

Take 1lb. each diced of potatoes, cauliflower, swedes, and carrots, three or four spring onions—if possible, one teaspoonful of vegetable extract, and one tablespoonful of oatmeal. Cook all together for 10 minutes with just enough water to cover. Stir occasionally to prevent the mixture from sticking. Allow to cool; put into a piedish, sprinkle with chopped parsley, and cover with a crust of potato or wheatmeal pastry. Bake in a moderate oven until the pastry is nicely browned and serve hot with a brown gravy.

Lord Woolton, the business magnate who, until the war began, had 'no time for politics,' has kept Britain fed for three and a half years. Appointed Minister of Food in April 1940, he became responsible for feeding 41million people in Britain as well as looking after the 532 million citizens of the British Empire. Britain produced less than a third of the food it consumed and whilst the Ministry worked on huge logistics internationally and reformed agriculture here, Lord Woolton also targeted the 'people at home'.

He launched the National Food Campaign, urging people to make weaker tea - 'one for you, one for me and none for the pot' saved 50 shiploads of tea per annum - and never to peel potatoes. He was a superb team leader and quickly had the Ministry working at full capacity, particularly on propaganda. Soon Britain was awash with posters proclaiming, 'Waste Not, Want Not', 'Grow Your Own' and 'Eat Up Your Greens'. With meat and eggs severely rationed and citrus fruits only rarely available, Woolton was aware that people needed more than veg. Children and the poor were particularly vulnerable. His solution was free school meals and milk for 650,000 youngsters and the 'British Restaurant'- a nation-wide scheme of basic cafes, often run by volunteers, offering cheap, nutritious meals. For 8d you could tuck into a plate of meat and veg, with bread and a pudding.

Perhaps the most influential marketing ploy was a radio programme, broadcast six days a week after the morning news, aimed primarily at housewives and entitled 'The Kitchen Front', in which well-known cooks offered advice and cheap but sustaining recipes. One was 'Woolton Pie', a veg mixture thickened with oatmeal and topped with pastry and however unappetising it may have been, 'Woolton Pie' became famous as a symbol of British wartime resilience.

Nov 19ᴛʜ-25ᴛʜ 1943

IN THE NEWS

Friday 19   **"The Africa Star"** When you see a Serviceman or woman wearing this ribbon, pale buff with a central wide red stripe and two narrower stripes, one dark blue and the other light blue, you will know they took part in the great victory of Africa.

Saturday 20   **"Save Your Tyres"** The manufacture of synthetic rubber in America has not reduced the need for economy. The largest consumption of rubber is for large tyres on omnibuses, lorries and aeroplanes and crude rubber will still be needed.

Sunday 21   **"Miners on Mosley"** Miners leaders warned of serious repercussions in the coal industry. How can the Government square sending boys to prison for refusing to work underground with the release, as we fight against fascism, of the former fascist leader?

Monday 22   **"Saris Are No1 Christmas Gift"** Saris are replacing silk stockings for wives and sweethearts at home of British and US Servicemen in India. Made of silk and elaborately embroidered it might cost £50, or merely of cotton costing a shilling or two.

Tuesday 23   **"New Governor General"** The King has approved the appointment of the Duke of Gloucester as the Governor General of the Commonwealth in Australia when Lord Gowrie steps down next year.

Wednesday 24   **"Opening of Parliament"** At an appropriately subdued ceremony in the beautiful and compact Chamber, with carved roof and mural paintings, which is for the time being the House of Lords, the King opened the fifth war time session of Parliament.

Thursday 25   **"Thanksgiving Day"** For the second year in succession, the Stars and Stripes flew over Westminster Abbey whilst, inside, hundreds of American citizens, most of them members of the Armed Forces, were observing Thanksgiving Day.

HERE IN BRITAIN
"Russian Rubber Dandelions"

An experiment has been taking place at Kew Gardens to develop additional sources of rubber. Seeds of three plants, from which rubber has been produced in Russia, have been cultivated. The most promising is Koksaghyz, a dandelion which comes from the Ukraine and Poland and seems capable of giving a yield of 65 to 100 lb of rubber to the acre, compared with 800 to 1,000 lb an acre of Para rubber. It needs good soil and, moreover, a great deal of hand-weeding, which is extremely expensive here. In Russia this is done by women and children on collective farms.

AROUND THE WORLD
"Boston's Celebrations"

Boston has a close interest in Thanksgiving Day. There were Boston men in the Mayflower, more followed during the Puritan exodus and it was the Pilgrim Fathers who in thanks to God began that thanksgiving which has become so important. This year American soldiers, airmen, and nurses marched through the town accompanied by all branches of the home defence services. All Boston and the countryside had crowded the streets to greet the American visitors and they threw open their homes with traditional hospitality to all Americans who made the pilgrimage.

THE ARCTIC CONVOYS

ARMS FOR RUSSIA . . . A great convoy of British ships escorted by Soviet fighter planes sails into Murmansk harbour with vital supplies for the Red Army.

Mrs Churchill opened the Arctic Convoy Exhibition in London. It is designed to give the public an impression of the scope and growth of her 'Aid to Russia' Fund and she spoke of the valour and endurance shown by the men of the Royal and Merchant Navies in taking medical and surgical supplies, valued at nearly £3,000,000, to our ally.

More than 4,000 tons of supplies have already arrived in Russia and a great deal more is on its way. The goods sent by the Fund had been packed away among over 3,000 aircraft, nearly 3,000 tanks, over 30,000 lorries and cars and miscellaneous cargo weighing nearly 940,000 tons. Under the protection of the Royal Navy, hundreds of merchant ships carried these supplies in the teeth of the most bitter and desperate attacks from the great German cruisers sheltering in the Norwegian fjords, from the event more dangerous and certainly more active U-boats lurking in the path of the convoys, and from strong forces of the Luftwaffe.

In winter our ships had often been locked in ice and weighed down with ice amounting to as much as 150 tons. Sometimes there were 70deg of frost. In summer there was perpetual daylight, so that there was no relief from bombing. Mrs Churchill said our ships and men were under the incessant gaze of the enemy *'like an insect in a glass case'*. For security reasons she could not tell how many men had perished, but since the first convoy sailed for North Russia in August 1941, 750 officers and men of the two navies had been decorated for valour, gallantry, and endurance. The exhibition enables the public for the first time to witness the results of its generosity, actual specimens being shown of the medical and surgical supplies sent to our ally.

Nov 26th - Dec 2nd 1943

IN THE NEWS

Friday 26 — **"Toys and Games for Christmas"** Quota restrictions have been removed to make as many toys as possible available for Christmas. The maximum price of 24s 6d (£1.23) and the ban on metal toys remain in force.

Saturday 27 — **"Azores Pineapples"** A crowd gathered outside a London fruit shop where two fresh pineapples were exhibited. They were the first arrivals from the Azores and priced at £6 each. The shopkeeper said he preferred to keep them as showpieces.

Sunday 28 — **"Flu Sweeps the Country"** An epidemic is sweeping the country. Doctors say it has struck much earlier than usual but fortunately, so far, most of the cases have not been severe.

Monday 29 — **"Non-Stop Open Fire"** An open grate which burns continuously, with little smoke and from which the ashes must be removed only once a week, is being developed by the British Coal Utilisation Research Association.

Tuesday 30 — **"Hospitals to Lose More Medical Staff"** To meet the expected urgent demands of the services, 50% of the newly qualified doctors will receive their calling up papers within a few days. Every hospital is already struggling along with less than half its peace-time medical staff.

Weds Dec 1 — **"Atlantic Flight Record"** A B24 Liberator on the RAF Transport Command North Atlantic shuttle ferry for BOAC, has made a non-stop flight of 3,100 miles from Montreal to the west coast of Britain in 11 hours 35 minutes.

Thursday 2 — **"Men For the Mines Compulsion"** Because voluntary recruitment measures have not worked, the Government has decided that some thousands of men between 18 and 25, who would otherwise go to the services, must now be 'directed' to the mines.

HERE IN BRITAIN
"Victory Potato"

A parcel bearing purple and blue Canadian stamps and labelled 'Fragile,' 'Handle with care,' and 'Do not crush,' reached the office of The Times and in it was no ordinary potato. Instead of the usual oval shape this potato is an almost perfect V, grown by a Scot in British Columbia. As a potato it is impressive enough, it weighs 1lb 9oz, and each arm of the V is more than 6in long, but it is as a unique form of the V sign that it has been sent to London with the request that it be forwarded to the Prime Minister.

AROUND THE WORLD
"Earthquake in Turkey"

A violent earthquake shock occurred in the Anatolia region of northern Turkey this week. Much damage and loss of life was caused throughout almost the whole area and communications were interrupted.
Relief supplies were sent from Ankara to the stricken areas and reports reveal that more than 1,800 people were killed and 2,000 seriously injured in the earthquake but numbers may rise when reports come in from distant areas. Twenty-nine villages were completely destroyed, a 25-mile section of the Amasia-Samsun railway wrecked, and several highways disappeared.

EATING AT THE NATIONAL

The war years have seen music and good eating added to the pictures as attractions offered at the National Gallery. It is the National Gallery canteen which accounts for the long queue to be seen outside the gallery any weekday between midday and 3pm and this quite remarkable canteen has just celebrated its fourth birthday. The canteen is run by volunteers and started when people flocked to Dame Myra Hess's lunch hour concerts. They were working folk, many of them Civil servants from the neighbouring offices, and one day, a member of the audience, Lady Gater, realised how hungry she was and with one or two friends provided sandwiches and cartons of milk. Soon power was installed, and hot coffee became possible, then pots and pans were borrowed from friends and the first hot luncheon was cooked. Today the daily average of meals served is 1,460, and sometimes the figure is as high as 2,200. The canteen is open to Civil servants and all full-time war workers, and among its regular patrons are Ministers and permanent heads of departments, generals and admirals, and men and women of the British and allied forces.

Because it is so popular, eating is a somewhat crowded but thoroughly friendly affair and in the summer the diners overflow on to the lawn outside the gallery. The cramped conditions inside are, however, more than outweighed by the excellence of the fare provided which is due to the inventiveness of the volunteer cooks under the head cook, an amateur who, formerly an executive with a leading dressmaking house, is making the most of her experience as a consumer of the cooking in France and Italy before the war. In meeting a real demand, the canteen is proving an outstanding success financially – to the benefit of many charities.

IN THE NEWS

Friday 3   **"Minister Too Optimistic about Controlled Turkeys"** Mr Alan Sainsbury said, *"probably not more than one family in 10 will be able to purchase a turkey this Christmas."* Distribution should be on the same basis as meat and leave the rest to the retailers.

Saturday 4   **"Ex-Nurses Return"** Six thousand five hundred women were placed in nursing and midwifery vacancies in the five months to the end of October and the numbers are rising.

Sunday 5   **"Ploughs Rusting in the Port"** Farmers in Lincolnshire have been waiting two years for permits for ploughs to cultivate the 20,000 more acres a year the Government has asked for. Meanwhile, there are hundreds of ploughs waiting to be shipped to, as yet, unliberated countries.

Monday 6   **"Death to London Sewer Rats"** An onslaught against the brown rats begins today. Rats have been damaging food to the extent of 2,000,000 tons a year.

Tuesday 7   **"No Pearl Harbour Celebrations"** President Roosevelt has rejected a request for an 'Armed Services Honour Day' on the anniversary of Pearl Harbour. *'December 7 two years ago is a day that is remembered as one of infamy on the part of a treacherous enemy. The day itself requires no reminder.'*

Wednesday 8   **"Puddings for Christmas"** There will be more in the shops this year than last – because none will weigh more than 2lb. As there is unlikely to be enough to satisfy demand, there is an increase in supplies of biscuits.

Thursday 9   **"Help from Army Doctors"** The Ministry of Health is securing more medical aid to deal with the influenza epidemic. The call up of young doctors has been delayed and Service medical officers are to help.

HERE IN BRITAIN
"Canadian Wing"

A Canadian wing is to be built by the Dominion Government as part of the plastic and jaw injuries centre of a hospital in East Grinstead, Sussex, where many Canadian air crew suffering severe burns and disfiguring injuries have been restored to normal health.

Canada is providing the £18,000 which it will cost, and work has already been begun by units of the Royal Canadian Engineers. For the duration of the war the wing will house a plastic surgery unit of the Royal Canadian Air Force Medical Branch.

AROUND THE WORLD
"Kissing the Sword of Stalingrad"

This week the King's sword was presented to Marshal Joseph Stalin by Mr Churchill, in the presence of President Roosevelt. Churchill took the sword from a British lieutenant and turning to Stalin declared, *"I am commanded to present this sword of honour as a token of homage of the British people".*

Stalin kissed the scabbard and quietly thanked the British. He then offered the sword for inspection to the seated President who drew the blade and held it aloft, saying, *"Truly they had hearts of steel".* (In Russian, Stalin's name approximates to 'man of steel').

BEVIN'S 'BOYS' BALLOT

Training in the highly dangerous coal industry was taken seriously. The Bevin's Boys had both theoretical and practical training in underground coal mining.

Mr Bevin has decided the young men, aged 18 – 25, to be called up for the mines should be selected by ballot. A draw will be made from time to time of one or more of the numbers from 0 to 9, and those men eligible, whose National Service registration certificates happen to end with the figure or figures drawn, will be transferred to the coalmines. 30,000 men are needed before the end of next April.

If your name is called out of the hat, this is what will happen. You will be given at least four weeks training. 50% of your 44-hour week will be spent in physical training and classroom work, 30% on instruction below ground and the remaining 20% on surface work. An experienced miner will supervise your work during the first four weeks underground and unless you live in South Wales, you will not be sent to work at the coal face until you have had at least four months underground experience. You will be billeted in a miner's home or in a specially built hostel. You will receive a minimum wage ranging from 39s 6d (£1.97) at 17, to 78s (£3.40) at 21, with allowances for living away from home and when demobilisation comes, you will be dealt with exactly as though you were a soldier. Three classes of men will be excluded. Men accepted for flying duties in the RAF or Fleet Air Arm; men accepted as artificers in submarines and men in a short list of highly skilled occupations. Conscientious objectors will not be exempt.

The President of the South Wales miners said, *"I think the plan will work. It will get rid of the idea that young men who have volunteered for the mines, have done so to avoid military service."*

DEC 10TH - DEC 16TH 1943

IN THE NEWS

Friday 10 "Motorways of Future" An exhibition in London shows by means of diagrams, photographs and working models, the advantages of roads, 100ft wide, divided into two 30ft one-way carriage ways by a centre strip planted with flowering trees and shrubs, and only open to fast running motor traffic.

Saturday 11 "Flying Boat Smashes Record" The new US cargo flying boat 'Mars' has broken all records for aerial cargo and over-water flight. 'Mars' has made a 4,375-mile non-stop flight from Washington to Natal in Brazil, carrying 13,000 lb of Christmas mail for the armed forces.

Sunday 12 "The Campaign" The East Anglian sugar beet factories are in the middle of a spell of furious effort during which work goes on day and night for about 110 days. During this time, they produce some 500,00 tons of fine white sugar.

Monday 13 "Cancer Cure Will Save Thousands" For the first time in history, it is possible to state that one form of cancer, cancer of the prostate, can be completely controlled and the patient rendered symptom free by taking a few pills each day.

Tuesday 14 "Aircraft Production or Land Girls?" The demands of aircraft production and food will have to be balanced by the Ministry of Labour before they can decide whether they can spare more girls for the Land Army. At least 30,000 are wanted by farmers for next year.

Wednesday 15 "The First Ballot" A junior member of staff at the Ministry of Labour drew the first two numbers in the ballot for the direction of young men to the coal mines. The first training sessions will begin in January.

Thursday 16 "Mr Churchill Has Pneumonia" The Prime Minister is in Cairo for discussions with President Roosevelt and President Chiang Kai-Shek of China. He has been in bed in a private villa for some days and doctors say, at present, there is no case for undue worry.

HERE IN BRITAIN
"Airgraphs Going Nowhere"

Each week the Airgraph Section of the GPO is receiving some 2,000 airgraphs bearing no address, 210 airgraphs stamped and addressed but without any message, and 150 properly stamped forms but with no word written on them!

The other frequent mistakes are folding the forms unnecessarily small, usually into eight, meaning they must be smoothed out before going through the photographing machines or sticking a photograph of themselves or the baby on the form which makes it too thick for the machine.

AROUND THE WORLD
"Paintings Home to New York"

After 'responsible authorities' expressed their belief that the danger of a bombing attack is now past, the Metropolitan Museum of Art has been bringing back to the City, many of their valuable paintings which have been stored in a bomb-proof shelter on a private estate more than 100 miles away.

Several hundred are already back, including paintings from the collection of the late George Blumenthal, New York City's own collection of 82 paintings, valued at several million dollars and noted for its many fine portraits of notable Americans by American artists.

AIR ROUTES EXPANDING

(Top) A RAF Vickers Wellington Mk XIV, undergoing servicing at Lajes, Azores, airfield during WWII.

(Left) Keflavik airport, Iceland.

Since the outbreak of war, great sums of money have been spent by Britain in developing new air routes, extending small airfields, and creating new strategic bases. Though this work has been carried out entirely for war purposes, the new facilities will be of great value for post-war air transport.

In Africa, a reinforcement route running across the continent from Takoradi in the west to the Middle East, cost between £1,500,000 and £2,000,000 and 40 airfields, flying-boat bases and landing grounds have been provided in the four West African Colonies. Since the enemy were expelled from Africa, many airfields, badly smashed by allied bombing, have been virtually rebuilt and other airfields in Egypt and the Sudan, extended. More than £2,000,000 has been spent on extending the airfield at Gibraltar, which now has an 1,800 yards runway, extending for almost half its length out over the sea. In 1941 the British and Indian Governments decided to establish along the South Arabian coast, an alternative route for maintaining civil air communications between India and the Middle East and five small airfields have been extended.

On the two principal airfields in Iceland alone, the British Government has spent some £1,500,000. There are now on the islands, operational airfields for anti-U-boat purposes and convoy protection, and a transit base which is part of the chain of airfields linking Canada and the United States with Britain. Reykjavik now has four runways and there are many emergency landing bases for flying-boats and airplanes around the island. New bases have been created in the Azores and the air route to Australia has recently been restored from Ceylon. In Britain, £615,000,000 is allocated for the provision of a vast network of new airfields, camps and depots to accommodate the British and American Air Forces.

IN THE NEWS

Friday 17   **"Miss Baden-Powell's Birthday"** Great Britain's oldest Girl Guide, sister of the late Lord Baden-Powell, celebrated her 85th birthday at a party given for her by the Boys Scouts.

Saturday 18   **"Mrs Churchill Flies Across War Zone"** There has been no spread in the pneumonia and the improvement in the Prime Minister's general health has been maintained. Clementine Churchill, his wife, braved a cold and dangerous flight to be with him in Cairo.

Sunday 19   **"Foot and Mouth Disease"** The Ministry has ordered the counties of Derby, Leicester, Nottingham, Rutland and parts of Lincoln, the counties of Chester, Stafford and the West Riding of Yorkshire, Controlled Areas to prevent the spread of the disease.

Monday 20   **"Help in Fighting Influenza"** In view of the epidemic, the call up of pharmacists and dispensers has been suspended temporarily. Because of the exceptional demand for cough and cold medicines, a supplementary allocation of sugar has been granted to chemists and druggists.

Tuesday 21   **"Oranges for All – After Christmas"** More oranges are due to arrive from Spain and Palestine and between January and April next year, everybody in Britain should get at least one pound - three or four each.

Wednesday 22   **"Birthday of the Railway Companies"** A celebration luncheon was held for the 21st anniversary of the amalgamation of 120 individual railway companies into four great railway systems – the Great Western, London Midland and Scottish, London and North Eastern and Southern.

Thursday 23   **"Peak Christmas Mail"** Soldiers are giving invaluable help in 'Heartbreak Corner', a temporary parcel sorting office in London where they solve the problem of badly packed parcels – insufficient paper, weak string and lack of care - by repacking them neatly.

HERE IN BRITAIN

"Vanishing Hens"

Thieves from the towns, using motor transport, are carrying out large scale thefts of poultry in several parts of the country. These 'roost robberies' are carried out by moonlight and hundreds of people in the north of England who long ago booked their Christmas dinner from farmer friends, are being told that the birds have gone. From a homestead in the Lake District, 100 head of poultry vanished in one night and in one village a farmer's wife who went out in the morning to feed 30 geese, which for weeks she had been fattening, found the flock had gone.

AROUND THE WORLD

"US Trains Double Crash"

More than 50 people were killed were injured in the wreck of two express trains in a snowstorm near Buie in North Carolina. The last three coaches of the Tamiami East Coast Champion, bound from New York to Tampa, were derailed and thrown on to the opposite track, one person being killed. A further accident was immediately prevented by railwaymen and passengers signalling a second south-bound train to stop. But despite frantic efforts they were unable to stop the West Coast Champion which came speeding northwards a quarter of an hour later.

WRIGHT BROTHERS' 40TH

MACHINE THAT FLIES

WHAT THE WRIGHT BROTHERS' INVENTION HAS ACCOMPLISHED.

Americans Seem to Have Solved Problem of Aerial Flight—Air Navigated Without Aid of Balloon. Built on Aeroplane Plan.

From The Car.
THE WRIGHT MACHINE.

THE INVENTORS OF THE AEROPLANE.

The first flight of the Wright Flyer, December 17, 1903, Orville piloting, Wilbur at the wingtip.

Dayton, Ohio, celebrated the fortieth anniversary of the historic pioneer flight of the Wright brothers in a power-driver controlled aircraft. Wilbur Wright died in May 1912, but his brother Orville remains the most distinguished figure in aviation in America. Sir Archibald Sinclair, Secretary of State for Air, on behalf of the Royal Air Force, sent a message to Dayton: '*Everyone who is familiar with the experiments and inventions of the immortal Wright brothers knows the patience, skill, and determination with which they worked, regardless of their own safety and the indifference of contemporary opinion.*

On December 17, 1903, they triumphantly reached their goal. I believe I am right in saying that on this historic occasion the aircraft flew between 30 and 35 miles per hour. At more than 10 times that speed the lineal descendants of Mr. Wright's machine are fighting and smashing the German and Japanese enemies of civilisation. I am proud to offer the best wishes of the Royal Air Force to Mr Orville Wright, and to acclaim the conquest of the air with which he and his illustrious brother, the late Mr. Wilbur Wright, will be for ever associated'

At the Orville Wright anniversary dinner in Washington, a message from President Roosevelt was read which stated that Wright has ended his feud with the Smithsonian Institute and given permission for the return of his aeroplane to the Institute from the Science Museum in South Kensington, London.

The successful initial flights were made on December 17. The first, under the control of Orville Wright, covered 100ft in 12 seconds, the second, under Wilbur Wright, made 175ft. Orville covered 200ft on the third attempt and the final flight of the day was 852ft with a duration of 59 seconds.

DEC 24TH - DEC 31ST 1943

IN THE NEWS

Friday 24 **"Travel Warnings Ignored"** Although the public has been asked to stay at home this Christmas all London stations were crowded with those determined to go away.

Saturday 25 **"The King's Broadcast"** The King made his 6th Christmas broadcast to his 'Peoples at Home and in the Empire' - the fifth during the war.

Sunday 26 **"The Prime Minister's Progress"** Mr Churchill continues to make steady progress and is gathering strength. He is cheered by the large number of kind messages received during his illness from all parts of the world.

Monday 27 **"Postcards Arrived in Time"** Some 13,000 postcards from prisoners of war and civilian internees in Japanese hands reached this country in time for delivery by Christmas. The majority came from Malaya.

Tuesday 28 **"Together for Christmas"** 200 civilian workers from Gibraltar arrived in London on Christmas Eve to spend Christmas and the New Year with their evacuated families.

Wednesday 29 **"Free Gas Mask Repairs"** During January and February repairs will be free as a step to ensuring that the public's gas masks are maintained in efficient condition.

Thursday 30 **"Prime Minister to Recuperate in the Sunshine"** Mr Churchill issued a 'personal note' in which he told the country, *'I have not at any time had to relinquish my part in the direction of affairs, and there has been not the slightest delay in giving the decisions which were required from me. I am now able to transact business fully.'*

Friday 31 **"500,000 Sewer Rats Destroyed"** The campaign opened a fortnight ago is progressing well. The attack is being made in 3,000 miles of sewers.

HERE IN BRITAIN
"Christmas at Home"

In Britain it was one of the most peaceful war-time Christmases. Reassuringly, at 12-hour intervals came bulletins that there has been 'no enemy air activity.' The embargo having been lifted, the church bells rang out on Christmas Day and London heard the chimes of Westminster Abbey, St. Paul's Cathedral and St. Martin-in-the-Fields again. Christmas Day congregations in the churches were large, sometimes even crowded. Mingled among the civilians were many uniformed men and women from America and no friends from overseas were ever more welcome.

AROUND THE WORLD
"Troops of Five Nations"

An old Christmas custom was revived this year when the lifting of black-out regulations permitted an open-air carol service round a bonfire in Shepherds Fields, outside Bethlehem on Christmas eve. Hundreds of men and women from all the services made up the congregation and the singing was led by an RAF male choir from Haifa. Bethlehem itself was filled throughout the night with troops from all the allies and Nativity Square was lit up by an electrically illuminated cross.

CHRISTMAS MONEY

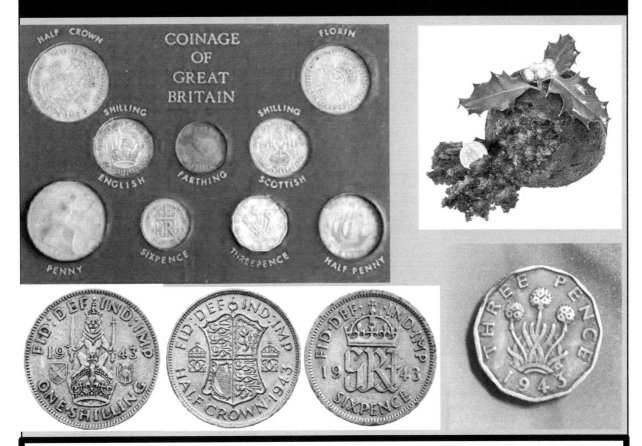

Christmas and new money are closely associated in the public mind. There is something very Christmassy about a new coin and its very brightness seems to add to its value as a Christmas box. The quantity of new money available varies from year to year, and this year there is plenty in circulation. The Royal Mint has been working double shifts to strike the large quantities of extra coin now required to pay the fighting services and the vast number of men and women on war work. The new money is therefore being sent where it is most needed, industrial and military centres, rather than residential areas.

At one time the Royal Mint, with the support of the banks, entered into the spirit of Christmas and made enough new money to supply all who wanted it, and some shopkeepers took so much that during Christmas week, all change was given only in new coin. This year it would put too much strain on bank's depleted staff and overload already overworked railways. Nor will many housewives have a 1943 silver threepenny bit to put in their puddings.

These little coins are out of favour and the Royal Mint, feeling that its real duty is to provide coin for spending and not for cooking, has concentrated instead on the production of the new yellow, 12-sided type. Vast quantities have been issued, but they are made of brass, and no housewife would care to boil them in her pudding! There are no new 5s pieces - none have been struck since the Coronation Year of 1937 - but other coins are in plentiful supply. The florin is maintaining its popularity and is largely used on pay-days in the services, and, as it is one-tenth of a pound, American soldiers, used to decimal coinage, seem to like it.

1943 Calendar

January

S	M	T	W	T	F	S
					1	2
3	4	5	6	7	8	9
10	11	12	13	14	15	16
17	18	19	20	21	22	23
24	25	26	27	28	29	30
31						

February

S	M	T	W	T	F	S
	1	2	3	4	5	6
7	8	9	10	11	12	13
14	15	16	17	18	19	20
21	22	23	24	25	26	27
28						

March

S	M	T	W	T	F	S
	1	2	3	4	5	6
7	8	9	10	11	12	13
14	15	16	17	18	19	20
21	22	23	24	25	26	27
28	29	30	31			

April

S	M	T	W	T	F	S
				1	2	3
4	5	6	7	8	9	10
11	12	13	14	15	16	17
18	19	20	21	22	23	24
25	26	27	28	29	30	

May

S	M	T	W	T	F	S
						1
2	3	4	5	6	7	8
9	10	11	12	13	14	15
16	17	18	19	20	21	22
23	24	25	26	27	28	29
30	31					

June

S	M	T	W	T	F	S
		1	2	3	4	5
6	7	8	9	10	11	12
13	14	15	16	17	18	19
20	21	22	23	24	25	26
27	28	29	30			

July

S	M	T	W	T	F	S
				1	2	3
4	5	6	7	8	9	10
11	12	13	14	15	16	17
18	19	20	21	22	23	24
25	26	27	28	29	30	31

August

S	M	T	W	T	F	S
1	2	3	4	5	6	7
8	9	10	11	12	13	14
15	16	17	18	19	20	21
22	23	24	25	26	27	28
29	30	31				

September

S	M	T	W	T	F	S
			1	2	3	4
5	6	7	8	9	10	11
12	13	14	15	16	17	18
19	20	21	22	23	24	25
26	27	28	29	30		

October

S	M	T	W	T	F	S
					1	2
3	4	5	6	7	8	9
10	11	12	13	14	15	16
17	18	19	20	21	22	23
24	25	26	27	28	29	30
31						

November

S	M	T	W	T	F	S
	1	2	3	4	5	6
7	8	9	10	11	12	13
14	15	16	17	18	19	20
21	22	23	24	25	26	27
28	29	30				

December

S	M	T	W	T	F	S
			1	2	3	4
5	6	7	8	9	10	11
12	13	14	15	16	17	18
19	20	21	22	23	24	25
26	27	28	29	30	31	

IF YOU ENJOYED THIS BOOK PLEASE LEAVE A RATING OR REVIEW AT AMAZON

Printed in Great Britain
by Amazon

de6bae18-df66-4246-a0e2-306619b63ccdR01